AMERICAN Arias

A Collection of Essential Contemporary Works

Voice: Baritone/Bass

BOOSEY & HAWKES

To Carolyn, for her constant support . . . and patience

TABLE OF contents

continued

TABLE OF contents

Concept & design: Lost In Brooklyn Studio www.lostinbrooklyn.com
Cover photography: © image100, Ltd.

FORWARD

About the Collection

Operas by Boosey & Hawkes composers have long provided recital and audition material for singers in search of English-language arias. The **American Arias** collection has been created with singers' needs in mind, offering selections to suit each voice and disposition. Each volume includes familiar arias and lesser known gems. I invite you to discover these works, and through them each composer's compelling creative voice.

I would like to also address the issue of American diction. In singing these American English arias, please be careful not to affect a foreign-sounding pronunciation, as it is inappropriate for much American material and makes singers sound unnatural; it also distracts the audience from experiencing the authenticity of the character and the story being presented.

Please note that some of the lengthier instrumental sections of certain arias have been edited for the purpose of this publication.

—Philip Brunelle

JOHN ADAMS

I WAS LOOKING AT THE CEILING AND THEN I SAW THE SKY
"Dewain's Song of Liberation and Surprise"

I Was Looking at the Ceiling and Then I Saw the Sky is a unique two-act "song play" that Adams wrote in 1995 to a libretto by the poet June Jordan. *Ceiling/Sky*, a romance, a comedy and a trenchant social satire, presents the lives of seven young men and women living in a poor neighborhood of Los Angeles, where they struggle against the hardships and paradoxes of their daily lives. A major earthquake hits the city, throwing their conflicts and loves into sharper relief—but also inspiring clarity and even consolation.

At the time of the earthquake, Dewain is in jail, facing trial for a petty offense that will nonetheless leave him incarcerated for most of his life if he is convicted. Sung from the ruins of his cell, which has been destroyed by the earthquake, "Dewain's Song of Liberation and Surprise" expresses the shock of sudden, literal freedom, which is itself transcended by the revelation of his innate freedom.

EL NIÑO
"Dawn Air"
"Shake the heavens"

El Niño (2000) tells the story of the Nativity, drawing its text from a variety of sources: New Testament gospels, Old Testament prophecies, little-known episodes from apocryphal texts, and 20th-century Mexican poetry (in both Spanish and English) that lends a contemporary resonance to the opera/oratorio.

"Dawn Air," written by Vicente Huidobro (1893–1948) and set here in a translation by David Guss, invokes majestic and natural imagery to convey a song of love and praise. "Shake the heavens" takes as its text three verses from the Old Testament book of Haggai. These words of God, a promise to shake the heavens, the earth, and the sea, are fearsome but ultimately celebratory of God's power to bring glory and peace to the earth.

NIXON IN CHINA
"News Aria"
"Chou En-lai's Epilogue"

John Adams's 1987 opera *Nixon in China* has become famous for its groundbreaking subject matter. President Richard Nixon's 1973 meeting with Chairman Mao Tse-Tung of China was a dramatic event in itself, signaling a new and cautious engagement between powerful nations. *Nixon in China*'s librettist, Alice Goodman, presents Nixon, Mao, their associates, and their spouses as complex individuals who find themselves in heroic circumstances. The eyes of the world are upon them, yet they cannot help but give voice to the dreams, anxieties, and memories aroused by these epochal events.

Nixon sings his first aria in the opera, "News has a kind of mystery," after stepping off Air Force One and meeting the Chinese Premier, Chou En-lai. With a nervous air of excited idealism, the President describes his exhilaration as he imagines himself at the forefront of history. Before long, however, he comes to dwell on anxiety and the weight of his task at hand.

The third act of the opera takes place during the last night of the visit, and finds all the characters fatigued and introspective. Chou En-lai's "Epilogue" closes the opera with a quiet meditation on old age, remorse, regret and the limitations of human actions.

DOMINICK ARGENTO

THE BOOR
"The Boor's Aria"

Dominick Argento's one-act opera buffa *The Boor* treats Anton Chekhov's play of the same title. One year after her husband's death, a widow still mourns him constantly, even though he used to leave her for days at a time to see his mistresses. Suddenly a man barges into her country house and demands that she immediately pay him a debt left by her husband, so that he can repay a bank loan the next day. The widow cannot give him the money until the day after, however, and refuses to think about the matter further because of her "state of mind" on the anniversary of her husband's death. She leaves the room curtly, and the boor sings his indignant aria: he is accused constantly of being a boor, but really it's other people who are always rude to him.

Ultimately the widow and the boor resolve to fight a duel. As they prepare their pistols, however, the boor becomes enamored of the widow's strength and spirit. Instead of a shot the duel comes to a kiss, and finally the widow is ready to live life again without mourning.

CASANOVA'S HOMECOMING
"Casanova's Final Air"

The exploits of Giacomo Casanova—the 18th-century Venetian traveler, scholar, swindler, writer, diplomat, gambler, entrepreneur, musician, and insatiable lover—could fill several comic operas. Argento's *Casanova's Homecoming* treats a couple of choice episodes set in 1774, when Casanova returns to Venice after twenty years of exile. To provide a dowry for Barbara, a former lover's daughter, Casanova extracts riches from a wealthy widow who believes in his supposed powers of the occult. Enlisting the help of his friends, he pulls off the swindle while slyly evading the city authorities, who suspect he is still up to no good.

After Barbara's wedding, Casanova leads the party in a toast to the bride and groom and then sings his "Final Air," which sums up the credo of his life, and of the opera: to live, to love, and to love living.

CHRISTOPHER SLY
"Sly's Aria"

The story of Christopher Sly, which serves as an introduction to Shakespeare's *The Taming of the Shrew*, stands on its own in Argento's one-act chamber opera. Sly has fallen into a drunken sleep outside an ale-house while fleeing his creditors, and he is chanced upon by a Lord and his hunting party. The Lord decides to play a joke on Sly, taking him to his manor and setting him in a luxurious bedroom. When Sly wakes up, the Lord and his servants try to convince him that he is really a lord himself, and his life as Christopher Sly was only a dream.

The dazed Sly realizes he has been tricked when he hears his creditors enter the manor. Asking for a minute of solitude, he grabs all the valuables he can reach and slips out the window, all the while singing his triumphantly spiteful aria.

THE MASQUE OF ANGELS
"Metatron's Sermon"

The one-act chamber opera *The Masque of Angels* presents a gathering of angels, who exist outside the earthly perception of time but are devoted to the cause of inspiring love among mortals. With choristers, musicians, and dancers in their ranks, the angels gather in a present-day church and await their leader, Metatron. Upon his arrival, Metatron informs the angels of the purpose of their gathering: "to encourage one mortal love." A young man and woman are at the focus of their efforts; they have met in the church, unsure of their love for each other. The angels, invisible to

them, lend them encouragement through song and dance, but still their message eludes the young couple. Finally, Metatron delivers to them his "Sermon"; although they cannot perceive him, the lovers absorb his words and speak his last thought for themselves: "There is joy in the company of God's angels."

THE SHOEMAKERS' HOLIDAY
"Simon's Aria"
"Ralph's Letter-Ballad"

The Shoemakers' Holiday is an adaptation of Thomas Dekker's play of the same name, written in London around 1600. A high-spirited celebration of virtue and good fortune, the story centers around the shop of Simon Eyre, the shoemaker of the Lord Mayor of London. Rowland Lacy, the Earl of Lincoln's nephew, is in love with Rose, the Lord Mayor's daughter. Neither the Earl nor the Mayor wish the two to wed, however, and they contrive to separate the lovers. Lacy is sent abroad to fight in the army, but deserts and returns to London in the guise of a Dutchman, working in Eyre's shop. Simon Eyre ascends to become Lord Mayor himself and, in that capacity, secures the King's blessing for Lacy and Rose to be wed.

Simon sings his aria upon his ascension to Lord Mayor, and it swirls with both excitement and a recognition that mad fortune, and not reason, has provided for his accomplishment.

Meanwhile, a subplot in the play follows Ralph Damport, one of Simon's shoemakers, who is conscripted into the army and separated from his young wife, Jane. Wounded and lonely, Ralph writes to Jane in a "Letter-Ballad," in which his sadness gradually gives way to an appeal for her constancy. Ralph's worries are prescient, as Jane, believing him to be dead, moves to a different part of London and allows herself to be courted by an unscrupulous city gentleman. Keeping in the spirit of the rest of the opera, however, Ralph manages to win her back from the brink of marriage—not without, of course, the help of good fortune.

A WATER BIRD TALK
"The Lecturer"

A Water Bird Talk, freely adapted by Dominick Argento from Chekhov's "On the Harmfulness of Tobacco" and Audubon's "The Birds of America," is a one-act monodrama tinged with humor and pathos. In the late 19th century, a middle-aged gentleman is delivering a lecture on water birds; the opera is sung as if directed towards the lecturer's audience. While describing the habits of various birds, in front of projected slides of Audubon's illustrations, he unwittingly draws parallels with his own life. The cormorant's young never leave the nest; the male phalarope attends to domestic duties while the female flits about. Ultimately he reveals himself as an unhappy man, henpecked by his wife and laughed at by his daughters.

The beginning of his speech, included in the aria "The Lecturer," immediately evinces his nervousness and timid deference to his wife, who sits unsympathetically in the wings.

JACK BEESON

DR. HEIDEGGER'S FOUNTAIN OF YOUTH
"Prescription for Living"

Dr. Heidegger's Fountain of Youth, a one-act chamber opera adapted from a short story by Nathaniel Hawthorne, presents a moral lesson through a fantastic story set in 19th-century America. The elderly Dr. Heidegger invites four friends, all also very old, to his home to take part in an experiment. He produces a flask of water supposedly taken from the fabled Fountain of Youth, and each of his guests drink from it. They quickly regain their youth, but their youthful passions return as well. The two women and two men are soon fighting for each other's attentions, and the flask is knocked over and broken. As the water spills away, old age returns to Heidegger's startled and saddened guests.

Dr. Heidegger's "Prescription for Living" is his lesson from the experiment: he will be satisfied in his old age and wisdom. His friends, however, pay no heed, and they vow to seek out the Fountain of Youth themselves.

HELLO OUT THERE
"The Gambler's Song"

Taking place entirely within the confines of a small-town jail in Texas, Jack Beeson's one-act chamber opera *Hello Out There* portrays a romance that blossoms quickly, only to end in heartbreaking tragedy hours later. A young man awakes behind bars in Matador, Texas, having been falsely accused of rape and then beaten in Wheeling, a nearby town. The only other person around is a young woman, the jail's cook, and the two are quickly drawn to each other. They each reveal their loneliness, and the gambler tells the girl he'll take her to San Francisco with him. In "The Gambler's Song," he sings hopefully of that future.

Afraid that the men from Wheeling will find him and kill him, the gambler sends the girl to fetch a gun. While she is gone, the men arrive and shoot him. The girl returns as he dies, and she sinks back into loneliness again.

LEONARD BERNSTEIN

MASS
"A Simple Song"

Leonard Bernstein's *Mass* (1971) is based on the Roman Catholic Mass, as seen from the point of view of a Celebrant who is experiencing a crisis of faith. It follows the liturgy exactly, but the liturgical passages are juxtaposed against frequent interruptions and commentaries by the Celebrant and the congregation, much like a running debate.

The Celebrant's faith is simple and pure at first, as shown in his wish to sing "A Simple Song" in praise of God. Yet that faith gradually becomes unsustainable under the weight of human misery, corruption, and the trappings of human power. In the end, the Celebrant, on the verge of renouncing his faith, finds that the loneliness of his doubt is no match for the joy of gathering together with other believers in praise.

TROUBLE IN TAHITI
"There's a law"

Leonard Bernstein's one-act opera *Trouble in Tahiti*, written on his own libretto in 1951, shows the anguish and loneliness present in the lives of a husband and wife who outwardly appear to be living out the American dream. The plot follows the arguments and frustrations of a single day out of their life, while a trio of jazz singers extols the virtues of family life in suburbia.

Sam has been married to Dinah for nearly ten years, and the two of them have a nine-year-old son, who this afternoon is playing the lead role in his school play. Sam, despite Dinah's arguments with him, insists on skipping the show and instead playing in a handball tournament at his gym. Afterward in the locker room, having won the handball trophy, Sam sings his aria "There's a law." With enraptured cockiness, and temporarily oblivious to the way he's distancing himself from his family, Sam declares that he's one of the winners in life.

CARLISLE FLOYD

COLD SASSY TREE
"Rucker's Sermon"
"I've known I've loved you"

Carlisle Floyd's opera *Cold Sassy Tree*, based on the novel by Olive Ann Burns, centers on Rucker Lattimore, a stubbornly idiosyncratic storeowner and grandfather. In the town of Cold Sassy Tree, Georgia, in 1900, Rucker has recently seen his wife through a long illness to her death. He shocks his family three weeks later by announcing his marriage to Love Simpson, a milliner at his store and a woman half his age. Reassuring them, he explains that theirs will be a "name only marriage"—she will take care of him, and in return she will be willed his house and furniture.

Though Rucker's family comes to tolerate his marriage to Love, barely, the other residents of Cold Sassy Tree are openly disgusted with the situation. When Rucker sends his grandson, Will, to church with Love for the first time, the congregation is openly hostile; Love and Will leave immediately. Back at home, Rucker decides to conduct his own church service, just for Love and his admiring grandson. "Rucker's Sermon" outspokenly delivers his beliefs about narrow-minded religious zealots, then concludes with an affirmation of God's desire for men and women to value and savor their lives.

The name-only marriage continues congenially, and after a while Rucker even surprises Love by installing indoor plumbing in the house—an expense he had stubbornly refused to make for some time. Touched by Love's happy reaction, Rucker finally feels moved to admit his feelings for her: in his aria "I've known I've loved you," he confesses that he's loved her from the start, and that he wants her to be a real wife to him.

OF MICE AND MEN
"George's Aria"

Of Mice and Men is Carlisle Floyd's operatic adaptation of John Steinbeck's classic 1937 novel. In the northern California of the Great Depression, two migrant workers, George Milton and Lennie Small, wander from job to job at different ranches. Lennie is a massive man, but too slow-witted to realize his strength; George is his loyal and longtime caretaker. Their one dream is to someday own a farm together, but ultimately this is denied them as Lennie's dangerous strength leads him into tragedy.

Shortly after the pair arrives at a new bunkhouse, George discovers a newspaper ad for a farm cheap enough for them to afford after a month's work. The experienced foreman of the ranch, Slim, sees George poring over the ad and tries to dissuade him from believing in that dream, which he has seen many ranch hands pursue, resulting only in bitter disappointment. George responds with his vehement aria, in which he forcefully insists that he and Lennie will find something more in their lives than wandering and loneliness.

THE PASSION OF JONATHAN WADE
"Sleep, conscience, sleep"

Set in the blackened ruin of Columbia, South Carolina, at the end of the Civil War, Carlisle Floyd's *The Passion of Jonathan Wade* is a tragedy of one man's life torn apart by the same forces that threaten the uneasy reconstruction of the South. Jonathan Wade, a colonel in the Union army, arrives in Columbia as the officer in charge of overseeing the city. He struggles, on one hand, with intransigent Rebels pledging violence; and on the other, Northern politicians exploiting the situation for their own political control. Meanwhile, he falls in love with Celia Townsend, the daughter of a local judge.

When Jonathan is instructed by Washington to remove Judge Townsend from his post, he is particularly torn. In obeying the command, he will betray Celia, as well as the Judge himself, who has been hospitable and generous to him. In "Sleep, conscience, sleep," Jonathan beseeches his conscience to stop tormenting him about the duty he must perform.

SUSANNAH
"Hear me, O Lord"

Carlisle Floyd's *Susannah*, more than any other opera, has come to represent the American South on stages across this country and overseas. In the mountains of Tennessee, in the mid-twentieth century, Susannah Polk lives with her brother Sam in the secluded community of New Hope Valley. Susannah's youth and radiant beauty cause the people around her—including the fiery Reverend Olin Blitch, a recent arrival to their church—to distrust her innocence. After she is spied bathing in a creek, the church elders viciously accuse her of being an evil adulteress, and she is made an outcast in the community. Reverend Blitch comes to Susannah's house to pressure her into repentance, but instead consummates his own desire for the girl, who is too distraught and exhausted to resist.

Blitch sings his Prayer of Repentance the next morning, alone in his church, as too late he realizes Susannah's innocence and the weight of his own sin. When his congregation arrives, he pleads with them to ask Susannah for forgiveness—though he does not admit his intimacy with her—but they refuse to believe in her innocence. Forgiveness is not to be had as Sam, returning from a hunting trip, hears Susannah's story and kills Blitch in a fit of rage.

WILLIE STARK
"Single bed blanket"
"We all come out of the earth"

Willie Stark is Carlisle Floyd's adaptation of Robert Penn Warren's novel *All the King's Men*, which tells of the rise and fall of a powerful governor in the deep South. Stark is loved by the rural poor for his populist convictions, hated by the state political machine for his ruthless maneuvering. Stark's titanic political stature is equaled by the overwhelming presence his personality commands in the lives of those close to him.

A heated battle is taking place in the state capitol, as Stark's political enemies fight to launch impeachment proceedings against him, based on Stark's manipulation of the state judicial system for the sake of his social reforms. When Stark hears that the highly respected Judge Burden is preparing to endorse the case for impeachment, he pays a visit to his home in order to dissuade him. The Judge's response is short but incisive: he will support the impeachment because of Stark's "contempt for the law." Stark responds with the aria "Single bed blanket," framing his own populist view of the law in the form of a folksy parable.

Later that same day, during a rally on the courthouse steps of his hometown of Mason City, Stark is suddenly moved by the sight of a young boy with a harmonica in the crowd. Reminded of himself in his own youth, Stark buys the harmonica from the boy and sings "We all come out of the earth." Losing his usual politician's toughness, Stark recollects his life's journey and realizes that he is homesick for the vision of himself that he has left behind.

DOUGLAS MOORE

THE DEVIL AND DANIEL WEBSTER
"I've got a ram, Goliath"

The Devil and Daniel Webster, set in New Hampshire in the 1840s, famously pits the Devil against the brilliant American lawyer and statesman. Webster is the guest of honor at the wedding of Jabez Stone, a state senator who had mysteriously managed to rise out of persistent poverty. The festivities are interrupted by the sinister Scratch, who in time reveals himself to be the Devil. Jabez admits that he sold his soul ten years beforehand, but Webster offers to argue his case. Scratch's hand-picked jury, made of infamous traitors brought back from hell, thwarts Webster's legal arguments, but even they are won over by his final appeal to life and freedom. Jabez Stone is

married, and the jubilant locals run the Devil out of New Hampshire.

In his aria "I've got a ram, Goliath," Webster sings of his strength as a farmer and his determination to stand up for freedom.

NED ROREM

THE ROBBERS
"I cannot still the echo"

Ned Rorem's *The Robbers* is a chamber opera in one scene adapted from the Pardoner's Tale from Chaucer's *Canterbury Tales*. Three highwaymen have lured a stranger into a room in an inn, where they have killed him for his gold. One of the robbers is young and inexperienced, and he is shaken by the murder. The other two, motivated by greed and also worrying that the novice may inadvertently give away the crime, plot to kill him later in the night.

Meanwhile, the novice continues to mull over the murder. In his aria "I cannot still the echo," his worries are gradually blended with a sinister idea: if he kills the other two, all the gold will be his.

The novice poisons a bottle of wine, which he takes to his companions. They kill him and then drink, leaving the curtain to fall on four corpses and a scattered pile of gold.

IGOR STRAVINSKY

THE RAKE'S PROGRESS
"Nick Shadow's Aria"

Stravinsky wrote his brilliant neoclassical opera *The Rake's Progress* in 1951 while he was living in Hollywood. W.H. Auden's libretto tells the story of Tom Rakewell, an idle young man who resolves to let fortune guide his life, rather than merit. When the sinister Nick Shadow arrives with news of an inheritance from an unknown uncle, Tom goes with him to London, intending to settle his affairs and then to send for his sweetheart Anne Trulove. Instead, Tom's weak character leaves him easy prey for Shadow, who guides him to self-destructively abandon all virtue.

After a little while in London, Tom becomes dissatisfied and unhappy. Shadow makes him an unlikely proposition: Tom should marry Baba the Turk, a bearded lady famous across Europe. Tom reacts incredulously, but Shadow convinces him of the plan with a devious aria: men are unhappy because they are not free, and to be free, they must abandon both reason and desire.

JOHN ADAMS

I WAS LOOKING AT THE CEILING AND THEN I SAW THE SKY
« Dewain's Song of Liberation and Surprise »

I Was Looking at the Ceiling and Then I Saw the Sky est un « chant-pièce » en deux actes, unique en son genre, écrit en 1995 par Adams, sur un livret composé par la poétesse June Jordan. *Ceiling/Sky*, à la fois histoire d'amour, comédie et satire sociale acérée, raconte la vie de sept jeunes gens dans un quartier pauvre de Los Angeles tandis qu'ils se débattent parmi les difficultés et les paradoxes de leur vie quotidienne. Un tremblement de terre de grande ampleur frappe la ville, soulignant davantage leurs conflits et leurs amours, cependant qu'il leur apporte aussi la clarté et même la consolation.

Lorsque le séisme se produit, Dewain est en prison, attendant d'être jugé pour un délit mineur qui le fera néanmoins rester en prison pendant la plus grande partie de sa vie s'il est condamné. Des ruines de sa cellule, détruite par le tremblement de terre, Dewain chante sa libération et sa surprise et exprime le choc éprouvé devant sa liberté matérielle soudaine, transcendée par la révélation de sa liberté intérieure.

EL NIÑO
« Dawn Air »
« Shake the heavens »

Le livret d'*El Niño* (2000) raconte l'histoire de la Nativité, en s'inspirant de sources diverses : Évangiles du Nouveau Testament, prophéties de l'Ancien Testament, épisodes peu connus tirés de textes apocryphes, et poésie mexicaine du XX siècle (à la fois en anglais et en espagnol), qui donnent une saveur contemporaine à l'opéra/oratorio.

« Dawn Air », écrit par Vicente Huidobro (1893–1948), chanté ici dans une traduction de David Guss, évoque des images majestueuses, liées à la nature, pour exprimer un chant d'amour et de louange. Le texte de « Shake the heavens » est constitué de trois versets du livre d'Aggée dans l'Ancien Testament. Ces paroles divines qui promettent d'ébranler les cieux, la terre et la mer, sont effrayantes, mais elles célèbrent en fin de compte la puissance de Dieu, capable d'apporter la gloire et la paix sur la terre.

NIXON IN CHINA
« News Aria »
« Chou En-lai's Epilogue »

L'opéra de John Adams, *Nixon in China* écrit en 1987, doit sa célébrité au caractère inédit du sujet traité. La rencontre du président Nixon avec le président chinois Mao Tsé-Toung en 1973 était en elle-même un évènement spectaculaire, annonçant l'avènement d'un engagement prudent entre de puissantes nations. La librettiste de *Nixon in China*, Alice Goodman, présente Nixon, Mao, leurs collaborateurs et leurs épouses, comme des personnalités complexes qui se sont trouvées dans des circonstances héroïques. Le monde a les yeux fixés sur eux, ce qui ne les empêche pas d'exprimer les rêves, les angoisses, et les souvenirs qu'ont suscités ces évènements d'importance historique.

Nixon chante le premier air de l'opéra « News has a kind of mystery » après être descendu de l'avion présidentiel en rencontrant le Premier ministre chinois Zhou Enlay. Manifestant un idéalisme fébrile, le Président décrit l'euphorie qu'il éprouve en se voyant jouer un rôle historique de premier plan. Cependant, il en vient bientôt à s'appesantir sur son angoisse et le poids que représente la tâche à accomplir.

Le troisième acte de l'opéra se passe pendant la dernière nuit de la visite et montre tous les personnages fatigués, s'interrogeant sur eux-mêmes. Avec l'épilogue de Zhou Enlay, l'opéra se termine par une méditation tranquille sur la vieillesse, le remords, le regret et les limites des actions humaines.

DOMINICK ARGENTO

THE BOOR
« The Boor's Aria »

L'opéra bouffe en un acte de Dominick Argento, *The Boor*, traite du sujet de la pièce du même nom d'Anton Tchekhov. Un an après la mort de son mari, une veuve porte toujours constamment son deuil, bien qu'il l'ait souvent quittée jadis pendant plusieurs jours pour rendre visite à ses maîtresses. Soudain, un homme fait irruption dans sa maison de campagne et lui demande de rembourser immédiatement une dette que son mari a contractée, pour qu'il puisse rembourser un prêt bancaire le lendemain. Cependant, la veuve ne peut pas lui donner l'argent avant le jour suivant, et refuse d'accorder davantage d'importance à cette affaire en raison de l'état d'esprit qui est le sien lors de l'anniversaire de la mort de son mari. Elle quitte la pièce sèchement et l'ours chante son indignation : on l'accuse toujours d'être un ours alors que ce sont les autres qui se conduisent toujours grossièrement avec lui.

Finalement, la veuve et l'ours décident de se battre en duel. Cependant, pendant qu'ils fourbissent leurs pistolets, l'ours s'éprend de l'énergie et de la force d'âme de la veuve. Le duel ne s'achève pas par des coups de feu, mais par un baiser, et la veuve est de nouveau prête à vivre sa vie sans être en deuil.

CASANOVA'S HOMECOMING
« Casanova's Final Air »

Les exploits de Giacomo Casanova—ce voyageur vénitien du XVIIIe siècle, érudit, escroc, écrivain, diplomate, joueur, entrepreneur, musicien et amant insatiable—pourraient remplir plusieurs opéras comiques. Dans *Casanova's Homecoming*, Argento traite de deux ou trois épisodes choisis qui se passent en 1774, quand Casanova revient à Venise après vingt ans d'exil. En vue de constituer une dot à Barbara, la fille d'une ancienne maîtresse, Casanova soutire de l'argent à une riche veuve qui croit en ses prétendus pouvoirs sur les puissances occultes. Il demande à ses amis de l'aider et il mène à bien son escroquerie tout en évitant habilement les autorités de la ville qui se doutent qu'il mijote quelque chose de louche.

Après le mariage de Barbara, Casanova entraîne la noce à boire à la santé des mariés et chante ensuite son « Final Air » qui résume sa philosophie de la vie et celle de l'opéra. vivre, aimer et aimer vivre.

CHRISTOPHER SLY
« Sly's Aria »

L'histoire de Christopher Sly, qui sert d'introduction à *The Taming of the Shrew* de Shakespeare, constitue la substance de l'opéra de chambre en un acte d'Argento. Sly, plongé dans un sommeil d'ivrogne en dehors d'un estaminet, alors qu'il fuit ses créanciers, est remarqué par hasard par un seigneur et le groupe des chasseurs qui l'accompagnent. Le seigneur décide de faire une blague à Sly en l'emmenant dans son manoir et en l'installant dans une chambre somptueuse. Quand Sly s'éveille, le seigneur et ses domestiques essaient de le convaincre qu'il est lui-même réellement un seigneur, et que la vie qu'il a menée sous l'identité de Christopher Sly n'était qu'un rêve.

Hébété, Sly se rend compte qu'il a été dupé quand il entend ses créanciers entrer dans le manoir. Il demande à rester seul une minute, attrape tous les objets précieux sur lesquels il peut mettre la main et s'échappe par la fenêtre tout en chantant triomphalement l'air qui exprime sa méchanceté.

THE MASQUE OF ANGELS
« Metatron's Sermon »

L'opéra de chambre en un acte, *The Masque of Angels*, présente une réunion d'anges, qui existent en dehors de la perception terrestre du temps, mais se dévouent à la cause qui consiste à inspirer l'amour parmi les mortels. Comptant parmi eux des choristes, des danseurs et des musiciens, les anges se rassemblent dans une église d'aujourd'hui et attendent leur chef, Metatron. À son arrivée, Metatron annonce aux anges le but de leur réunion : « encourager un amour mortel ». Un jeune homme et une jeune fille sont la cible de leurs efforts ; ils se sont rencontrés à l'église et ne sont pas sûrs de leur amour l'un pour l'autre. Les anges, invisibles à leurs yeux, les encouragent par leurs danses et leurs chants, mais le jeune couple ne comprend toujours pas leur message. À la fin, Metatron leur fait son « Sermon ». Bien qu'ils ne puissent pas le voir, les deux amoureux s'imprègnent de ses paroles et énoncent pour eux-mêmes sa dernière pensée : « la joie règne en compagnie des anges de Dieu ».

THE SHOEMAKERS' HOLIDAY
« Simon's Aria »
« Ralph's Letter-Ballad »

The Shoemakers' Holiday est une adaptation de la pièce du même nom de Thomas Dekker, écrite à Londres, autour de 1600. L'histoire, qui célèbre joyeusement la vertu et la chance, est centrée sur la boutique de Simon Eyre, le cordonnier du lord-maire de Londres. Rowland Lacy, le neveu du comte de Lincoln, est amoureux de Rose, la fille du lord-maire. Le comte et le maire sont tous les deux opposés au mariage et s'arrangent pour séparer les amoureux. Lacy est envoyé à l'étranger pour combattre dans l'armée, mais il déserte et revient à Londres, déguisé en Hollandais, travaillant pour Simon Eyre. Simon Eyre grimpe dans l'échelle sociale pour devenir lord-maire. À ce titre, il s'arrange pour obtenir la bénédiction du Roi autorisant le mariage entre Lacy et Rose.

Le chant de Simon parle de son ascension au poste de lord-maire, et virevolte entre l'enthousiasme et l'admission que la fortune aveugle, non la raison, lui ont permis de parvenir à ce rang.

Pendant ce temps, une intrigue secondaire de la pièce montre Ralph Damport, un des cordonniers de Simon, enrôlé de force dans l'armée, qui se trouve séparé de Jane, sa jeune épouse. Alors qu'il est blessé et se sent seul, Ralph écrit à Jane une « Letter-Ballad » dans laquelle sa tristesse se transforme peu à peu en plaidoyer pour la fidélité de sa femme. Les soucis de Ralph sont prémonitoires, car Jane, le croyant mort, va habiter dans un autre quartier de Londres et se laisse courtiser par un citadin sans scrupules. Cependant, conformément à l'esprit qui anime le reste de l'opéra, Ralph, aidé par la chance comme il se doit, s'arrange pour la reconquérir alors qu'elle est sur le point de se marier.

A WATER BIRD TALK
« The Lecturer »

A Water Bird Talk, librement adapté de la pièce de Tchekhov « On the Harmfulness of Tobacco » et de « The Birds of America » d'Audubon par Dominick Argento, est un drame en un acte teinté d'humour et de pathos. Vers la fin du XIXe siècle, un home d'âge mur fait une conférence sur les oiseaux aquatiques ; l'opéra est chanté comme s'il était destiné au public du conférencier. Tout en décrivant les habitudes des différents oiseaux devant des projections des illustrations d'Audubon, il les met involontairement en parallèle avec sa propre vie. Les petits du cormoran ne quittent jamais le nid ; le phalarope mâle s'occupe des tâches domestique pendant que la femelle volète autour de lui. Il se révèle finalement être un homme malheureux, que sa femme mène par le bout du nez et qui est la risée de ses filles.

Le début de son discours, qui se trouve dans l'aria « The Lecturer », manifeste tout de suite sa nervosité et sa déférence timide vis-à-vis de sa femme qui se trouve dans les coulisses, sans lui montrer la moindre bienveillance.

JACK BEESON

DR. HEIDEGGER'S FOUNTAIN OF YOUTH
« Prescription for Living »

Dr. Heidegger's Fountain of Youth, un opéra de chambre en un acte, adapté d'une nouvelle de Nathaniel Hawthorne, donne une leçon de morale par le biais d'une histoire fantastique qui se situe dans l'Amérique du XIXe siècle. Le Dr Heidegger, un homme âgé, invite chez lui quatre amis, aussi âgés que lui, pour prendre part à une expérience. Il leur montre une petite bouteille d'eau censée provenir de la célèbre fontaine de Jouvence et demande à chacun de ses invités d'en boire un peu. Ils retrouvent rapidement leur jeunesse, en même temps que leurs passions juvéniles. Les deux hommes et les deux femmes sont bientôt en train de se disputer pour se faire écouter des autres et le flacon se renverse et se brise. Tandis que l'eau s'écoule, les invités de Heidegger sont tout surpris de voir revenir leur vieillesse.

La « Prescription for living » du Dr Heidegger est la leçon qu'il donne après l'expérience: il sera satisfait dans sa vieillesse et sa sagesse. Néanmoins, ses amis ne lui prêtent aucune attention et jurent d'aller à la recherche de la fontaine de Jouvence.

HELLO OUT THERE
« The Gambler's Song »

L'action de l'opéra de chambre en un acte de Jack Beeson, *Hello Out There*, se passe entièrement dans la prison d'une petite ville du Texas et dépeint une idylle qui s'épanouit promptement pour se terminer en tragédie poignante quelques heures plus tard. Un jeune homme s'éveille dans une cellule de la prison de Matador, Texas, après avoir été faussement accusé de viol et battu dans une ville voisine, Wheeling. La seule personne qui se trouve à proximité est une jeune femme, la cuisinière de la prison, et les deux jeunes gens ressentent bientôt une attirance mutuelle. Ils parlent tous les deux de leur solitude et le joueur dit à la jeune fille qu'il va l'emmener à San Francisco avec lui. Dans « The Gambler's Song », il exprime son espoir en pensant à cet avenir.

Comme il a peur que les hommes de Wheeling le trouvent et le tuent, le joueur envoie la jeune fille chercher un revolver. Pendant qu'elle est partie, les hommes arrivent et lui tirent dessus. La jeune file revient alors qu'il meurt et retombe dans sa solitude.

LEONARD BERNSTEIN

MASS
« A Simple Song »

La *Mass* de Leonard Bernstein (1971) repose sur la messe catholique romaine, vue par un célébrant en train de passer par une période de crise dans sa foi. Elle suit exactement la liturgie, mais les passages liturgiques sont juxtaposés aux interruptions et commentaires fréquents du célébrant et de la congrégation, comme si un débat s'était engagé.

La foi du célébrant est simple et pure de prime abord, comme le montre son désir de chanter « A Simple Song » de louange à Dieu. Cependant, cette foi est peu à peu ébranlée par le poids de la misère, de la corruption et des pièges de la volonté de puissance humaine. À la fin, comme le célébrant est sur le point de renoncer à sa foi, il s'aperçoit que la solitude qui accompagne le doute ne peut égaler la joie éprouvée à se rassembler dans la louange avec d'autres croyants.

TROUBLE IN TAHITI
« There's a law »

L'opéra en un acte de Leonard Bernstein, *Trouble in Tahiti*, écrit en 1951 sur son propre livret, met en évidence l'angoisse et la solitude dans la vie d'un couple qui, vu de l'extérieur, paraît vivre le rêve américain. L'intrigue nous montre les disputes et les frustrations qui interviennent pendant une seule journée de leur vie, tandis qu'un trio de chanteurs de jazz exaltent les vertus de la vie de famille en banlieue.

Sam et Dinah sont mariés depuis près de dix ans et ils ont un fils de neuf ans, qui doit tenir le rôle principal dans une pièce de théâtre jouée dans son école, cet après-midi. Malgré tout ce que Dinah peut lui dire, Sam s'obstine et au lieu d'aller voir la pièce, il va participer à un tournoi de handball dans son club de gym. Par la suite, dans les vestiaires, après avoir gagné le trophée de handball, Sam chante son air « There's a law ». Radieux, très content de lui, oubliant pour un moment qu'il est en train de s'éloigner de sa famille, Sam déclare qu'il est un des élus de la vie.

CARLISLE FLOYD

COLD SASSY TREE
« Rucker's Sermon »
« I've known I've loved you »

L'opéra de Carlisle Floyd, *Cold Sassy Tree*, d'après le roman d'Olive Ann Burns, se concentre sur Rucker Lattimore, un vieux commerçant, qui est aussi grand-père, original et entêté. En 1900, dans le village de Cold Sassy Tree, en Géorgie, Lattimore est resté au chevet de sa femme au cours de sa longue maladie dont elle est morte récemment. Sa famille est choquée quand il annonce trois semaines plus tard qu'il va épouser Love Simpson, modiste dans sa boutique, qui a la moitié de son âge. En rassurant sa famille, il explique que ce mariage n'aura de « mariage que le nom », qu'elle s'occupera de lui et qu'en retour, elle recevra la maison et les meubles en héritage.

Malgré que la famille de Rucker s'accommode à peine de son mariage avec Love, les autres habitants de Cold Sassy Tree sont ouvertement écœurés de cette situation. Quand Rucker envoie son petit-fils à l'église avec Love pour la première fois, la congrégation affiche ouvertement son hostilité et Love et Will quittent immédiatement l'église. De retour à la maison, Rucker décide d'organiser son propre office religieux, rien que pour Love et son petit-fils. Dans son « Sermon », Rucker exprime en toute liberté ses opinions sur les bigots à l'esprit étroits, puis affirme en conclusion, que Dieu désire que les hommes et les femmes savourent leurs vies et leur accordent de la valeur.

Le mariage qui n'a-de-mariage-que-le-nom se poursuit agréablement, et Rucker va jusqu'à surprendre Love en faisant installer l'eau courante dans la maison, une dépense qu'il avait obstinément refusée de faire depuis quelque temps. Touché par la joyeuse réaction de Love, Rucker se trouve finalement ému au point de reconnaître ses sentiments pour elle : en chantant « I've known I've loved you », il avoue qu'il l'aime depuis le début et qu'il veut la voir devenir véritablement son épouse.

OF MICE AND MEN
« George's Aria »

Of Mice and Men est l'opéra que Carlisle Floyd a composé d'après le célèbre roman de John Steinbeck, écrit en 1937. En Californie du nord, au moment de la grande Dépression, deux ouvriers itinérants, George Milton et Lennie Small, vont de fermes en fermes à la recherche d'un travail. Lennie est un grand costaud, mais son intelligence est trop limitée pour qu'il ait conscience de sa force. George s'occupe fidèlement de lui depuis longtemps. Ils rêvent de posséder un jour une ferme à eux deux, mais, en fin de compte, cela ne se réalisera pas car la force de Lennie est dangereuse et l'entraîne dans une tragédie.

Peu après leur arrivée dans un pavillon-dortoir, George trouve une petite annonce pour une ferme bon marché, qu'ils pourraient acheter après un mois de travail. Le contremaître de la ferme, Slim, un homme plein d'expérience, voit que George est en train d'étudier l'annonce et essaie de le dissuader de croire en ce rêve que beaucoup d'ouvriers agricoles poursuivent pour se retrouver cruellement déçus. George répond par un chant véhément dans lequel il répète avec force que Lennie et lui vont mener une vie où régnera autre chose que l'errance et la solitude.

THE PASSION OF JONATHAN WADE
« Sleep, conscience, sleep »

The Passion of Jonathan Wade de Carlisle Floyd, se passe dans les ruines calcinées de Columbia, en Caroline du Sud, à la fin de la guerre de Sécession. C'est la tragédie d'un homme dont la vie a été déchirée par les forces même qui menacent la difficile reconstruction du Sud. Jonathan Wade, colonel dans l'armée de l'Union, arrive à Columbia en qualité d'officier chargé de superviser la ville. Il lutte à la fois contre l'intransigeance des rebelles qui promettent la violence et d'un autre côté contre les politiciens nordistes qui exploitent la situation pour affermir leur propre pouvoir politique. Pendant ce temps, il s'éprend de Celia Townsend, la fille d'un juge du pays.

Quand Jonathan reçoit les ordres de Washington de retirer son poste au juge, il est particulièrement déchiré. En obéissant aux ordres, il trahit à la fois Celia et le juge lui-même, qui a toujours fait preuve d'hospitalité et de générosité à son égard. Dans le chant «Sleep, conscience, sleep », Jonathan supplie sa conscience de cesser de le tourmenter au sujet du devoir qu'il doit accomplir.

SUSANNAH
« Hear me, O Lord »

Susannah de Carlisle Floyd, plus que tout autre opéra, en est venu à représenter le Sud des États-Unis sur les scènes de ce pays et à l'étranger. Susannah Polk vit avec son frère Sam dans une commune retirée, la vallée de New Hope, dans les montagnes du Tennessee, au milieu du XXe siècle. La jeunesse et la beauté radieuse de Susannah amènent son entourage, y compris le flamboyant révérend Olin Blitch, récemment arrivé dans la paroisse, à mettre en doute son innocence. Après l'avoir espionnée alors qu'elle se baignait dans un ruisseau, les membres du Conseil paroissial l'accusent méchamment d'être une femme adultère maléfique, et la transforment en paria de la société. Le révérend Blitch vient chez elle, mais au lieu de la pousser à se repentir, il assouvit son propre désir pour la jeune fille, qui, dans son désarroi, n'a pas la force de lui résister.

Le lendemain matin, seul dans son église, Blitch chante sa prière de repentir, car il s'est rendu compte, trop tard, de l'innocence de Susannah et de son propre péché. Quand les membres de la congrégation arrivent, il les supplie de demander pardon à Susannah, sans toutefois admettre les rapports intimes qu'il a eus avec elle, mais ils refusent de croire en son innocence. Le pardon ne sera pas accordé car Sam, de retour d'une partie de chasse, apprend ce qui est arrivé à Susannah et tue Blitch dans un accès de rage.

WILLIE STARK
« Single bed blanket »
« We all come out of the earth »

Willie Stark est l'adaptation que Carlisle Floyd a fait du roman de Robert Penn Warren *All the King's Men*, qui raconte l'ascension et la chute d'un puissant gouverneur du Sud profond. Les pauvres habitants des campagnes aiment Stark pour ses convictions populistes ; la machine politique de l'état le déteste en raison de ses manigances sans scrupules. Sa dimension politique titanesque n'a d'égale que l'influence excessive que sa personnalité exerce sur les vies de ceux qui l'entourent.

Une batille acharnée se déroule dans la capitale de l'état alors que les ennemis politiques de Stark se débattent pour lancer une procédure de destitution envers lui, en raison de ses manipulations du système judiciaire de l'état pour la réalisation de ses réformes sociales. Lorsque Stark apprend que le très estimé juge Burden se prépare à se rallier à la cause de la destitution, il lui rend visite chez lui afin de le faire changer d'avis. La réponse du juge est courte mais mordante : il va appuyer la destitution parce que Stark « méprise la loi ». Stark lui répond en chantant « Single bed blanket », formulant ses propres opinions populistes sous la forme d'une parabole toute simple.

Un peu plus tard dans la journée, lors d'un rassemblement sur les marches du tribunal de sa ville, Mason, Stark est soudain ému à la vue d'un garçon avec un harmonica, dans la foule. Se rappelant ce qu'il était dans sa jeunesse, Stark achète l'harmonica du jeune garçon et chante « We all come out of the earth ». Abandonnant son habituelle dureté d'homme politique, Stark se souvient de la vie qu'il a menée jusque là et se rend compte qu'il a la nostalgie de cette vision de lui-même qu'il a laissée derrière lui.

DOUGLAS MOORE

THE DEVIL AND DANIEL WEBSTER
« I've got a ram, Goliath »

The Devil and Daniel Webster, se passe dans les années 1840 dans le New Hampshire, où cette pièce célèbre oppose le diable au brillant avocat et homme d'état américain. Webster est l'invité d'honneur au mariage de Jabez Stone, un sénateur de l'état, qui a mystérieusement réussi à sortir d'une pauvreté persistante. Les festivités sont interrompues par le sinistre Scratch, qui révèle le moment venu qu'il est le diable en personne. Jabez reconnaît qu'il a vendu son âme dix ans auparavant, mais Webster propose de plaider sa cause. Les jurés choisis par Scratch, un ramassis de traîtres infâmes ramenés de l'enfer, réduisent les arguments juridiques de Webster à néant, mais ils finissent par se laisser gagner par son ultime appel à la vie et à la liberté. Jabez Stone est marié et les habitants en liesse expulsent le diable du New Hampshire.

Dans son air « I've got a ram, Goliath », Webster chante sa force comme paysan et sa détermination de lutter pour être libre.

NED ROREM

THE ROBBERS
« I cannot still the echo »

L'opéra de chambre à une scène de Ned Rorem, *The Robbers*, est adapté du Pardoner's Tale (conte du Confesseur), tiré des *Canterbury Tales* de Chaucer. Trois bandits de grand chemin ont attiré un étranger dans une chambre d'auberge où ils l'ont assassiné pour lui voler son or. L'un des voleurs est jeune et sans expérience, et il est bouleversé par l'assassinat. Les deux autres, poussés par l'appât du gain et craignant que le novice ne révèle le crime involontairement, décident de le tuer plus tard dans la soirée.

Pendant ce temps, le novice continue de penser à l'assassinat. Quand il chante « I cannot still the echo », une idée sinistre se mêle peu à peu à ses soucis : s'il tue les deux autres, l'or sera entièrement à lui.

Le novice met du poison dans une bouteille de vin et l'apporte à ses compagnons. Ils le tuent et ensuite, boivent, et le rideau tombe sur quatre cadavres et une montagne d'or.

IGOR STRAVINSKY

THE RAKE'S PROGRESS
« Nick Shadow Aria »

Stravinsky écrivit *The Rake's Progress*, opéra néo-classique brillant, en 1951, alors qu'il vivait à Hollywood. Le livret de W.H. Auden raconte l'histoire de Tom Rakewell, un jeune oisif qui décide de se laisser guider par la chance, plutôt que de compter sur ses mérites. Quand le sinistre Nick Shadow arrive et lui annonce qu'il a hérité d'un oncle inconnu, Tom part pour Londres, avec lui, avec l'intention d'arranger ses affaires et de faire venir ensuite sa petite amie, Anne Trulove. Au lieu de réaliser ce projet, le caractère influençable de Tom fait de lui une proie facile pour Shadow, qui l'incite à se détruire lui-même en abandonnant toute forme de vertu.

Après avoir passé quelque temps à Londres, Tom se retrouve mécontent et malheureux. Shadow lui fait une propositions étonnante : Tom devrait épouser Baba la Turque, une femme à barbe célèbre dans toute l' Europe. Tom réagit de manière incrédule, mais Shadow le convainc d'adopter le plan par un air pervers : les hommes ne sont pas heureux parce que 'ils ne sont pas libres, et pour être libres, ils doivent renoncer à la raison et au désir.

JOHN ADAMS

I WAS LOOKING AT THE CEILING AND THEN I SAW THE SKY
„Dewain's Song of Liberation and Surprise"

I Was Looking at the Ceiling and Then I Saw the Sky ist ein einzigartiger „Song Play" in zwei Akten, den Adams 1995 zu einem Libretto von June Jordan schrieb. *Ceiling/Sky* ist eine Liebesgeschichte, eine Komödie und eine bissige, sozialkritische Satire zugleich. Es beschreibt das Leben sieben junger Männer und Frauen in einem armen Stadtteil von Los Angeles und ihren Kampf gegen die Beschwernis und die Widersinnigkeit des Alltags. Ein einbrechendes Erdbeben in der Stadt löst eine verstärkte Gegenüberstellung von Konflikt und Liebe aus, jedoch entspringt daraus Klarheit und sogar Trost.

Zur Zeit des Erdbebens befindet sich Derwain im Gefängnis. Sein Vergehen ist zwar unbedeutend, könnte ihn aber im Falle eines Schuldspruchs den Großteil seines Lebens hinter Gittern kosten. „Dewain's Song of Liberation and Surprise" wird aus der vom Erdbeben zertrümmerten Zelle gesungen und beschreibt den Schock der plötzlich erlangten Freiheit, und wie er mit der Offenbarung seiner inneren Freiheit transzendiert wird.

EL NIÑO
„Dawn Air"
„Shake the heavens"

El Niño (2000) erzählt die Geschichte der Geburt Christi und bezieht seinen Text von verschiedenen Quellen: neutestamentlichen Schriften, Prophezeiungen aus dem alten Testament, weniger bekannten Auszügen aus den Apokryphen und auch mexikanischer Poesie aus dem zwanzigsten Jahrhundert (auf Englisch und Spanisch), welche der Oper bzw. dem Oratorium ein zeitgenössisches Gefühl verleihen.

„Dawn Air" von Vicente Huidobro (1893–1948) und hier in einer Übersetzung von David Guss aufgeführt, beruft sich auf majestätische and natürliche Bilder, um ein Lied der Liebe und des Lobes zu vermitteln. Der Text von "Shake the heavens" stammt von drei Versen aus dem alttestamentischen Bibelbuch Haggai. Diese furchterregenden Worte Gottes, ein Versprechen Himmel, Erde und das Meer zu bewegen, feiern letztendlich Gottes Macht den Frieden und Herrlichkeit auf Erden zu bringen.

NIXON IN CHINA
„News Aria"
„Chou En-lai's Epilogue"

John Adams Oper *Nixon in China* aus dem Jahre 1987 ist aufgrund seiner bahnbrechenden Thematik berühmt geworden. Das Treffen Richard Nixons im Jahre 1973 mit dem Parteivorsitzenden Mao Tse-Tung war an sich ein dramatisches Ereignis und bedeutete den Anfang eines neuen und vorsichtigen Dialogs zwischen den Weltmächten. Librettistin Alice Goodman beschreibt Nixon, Mao, ihre Kollegen und Ehepartner als komplexe Menschen, die sich in heroischen Umständen befinden. Obwohl die Welt sie beobachtet, fühlen sich diese Menschen bewegt ihren Träumen, Ängsten, und Erinnerungen, die von den wegweisenden Ereignissen hervorgerufen werden, Ausdruck zu geben.

Nixon singt seine erste Arie „News has a kind of mystery" nachdem er von Air Force One herabsteigt und dem chinesischen Premier Tschou En-lai begegnet. Mit unruhiger Miene beschreibt der Präsident mit begeistertem Idealismus seine Freude sich im Vorfeld der Geschichte zu sehen. Bald darauf ergeht er in Angst und verweilt über das Gewicht seiner bevorstehenden Aufgabe.

Im dritten Akt der Oper, der vom letzten Abend des Besuches handelt, sind alle Figuren erschöpft und nachdenklich gestimmt. Die Oper endet mit Tschou En-lais „Epilogue", einer Meditation über Alter, Reue, Bedauern und die Beschränkungen menschlichen Handelns.

DOMINICK ARGENTO

THE BOOR
„The Boor's Aria"

Dominick Argentos komische Oper in einem Akt *The Boor* behandelt Anton Chekhovs gleichnamiges Stück. Ein Jahr nach dem Tod ihres Mannes trauert die Witwe noch ständig um ihn, obwohl er sie tagelang alleine ließ, um seine Geliebten zu sehen. Plötzlich platzt ein Mann in ihr Landhaus herein und verlangt die Begleichung der Schulden ihres Mannes, so dass er am nächsten Tag einen Kredit zurückzahlen kann. Sie kann dem Mann das Geld jedoch erst am folgenden Tag geben und weigert sich aufgrund ihrer Gemütsverfassung am Todestag ihres Mannes dem Thema weitere Aufmerksamkeit zu geben. Als sie das Zimmer abrupt verlässt, singt der Flegel entrüstet in seiner Arie darüber wie er ständig als Flegel bezeichnet wird, obwohl andere Leute ihn ständig unhöflich behandeln.

Der Flegel und die Witwe beschließen ein Duell auszutragen. Als sie jedoch ihre Pistolen vorbereiten ist der Flegel von der Kraft und des Mutes der Witwe angetan. Anstatt eines Schusses endet das Duell mit einem Kuss, und endlich ist die Witwe bereit ihr Leben erneut und ohne Trauer zu leben.

CASANOVA'S HOMECOMING
„Casanova's Final Air"

Giacomo Casanovas Heldentaten als venedischer Reisender, Gelehrter, Schwindler, Schriftsteller, Diplomat, Spieler, Unternehmer, Musiker und unersättlicher Frauenliebhaber aus dem 18. Jahrhundert bieten genug Stoff für mehrere komische Opern. Argentos *Casanova's Homecoming* handelt von einigen besonderen Vorfällen aus dem Jahre 1774, als Casanova nach zwanzig Jahren nach Venedig zurückkehrt. Um eine Mitgift für Barbara, die Tochter einer ehemaligen Geliebten zu schaffen, bezieht er Geld von einer reichen Witwe, die von seinen angeblichen okkulten Kräften überzeugt ist. Seine Freunde helfen ihm beim Schwindel und mit List entkommt er den Behörden, die annehmen, dass er noch immer Böses im Schilde führt.

Nach Barbaras Hochzeit gibt Casanova vor den Gästen die Festrede für die Braut und den Bräutigam. Dann singt er sein „Final Air", welches sein Credo und das der Oper zusammenfasst: leben, lieben, und das Leben lieben.

CHRISTOPHER SLY
„Sly's Aria"

Die Geschichte von Christopher Sly, die in Shakespeare's *The Taming of the Shrew* als Einleitung dient, ist in Argentos Kammeroper in einem Akt in sich abgeschlossen. Auf der Flucht vor seinen Gläubigern ist Sly im Rausch vor einem Wirtshaus eingeschlafen, wo er zufällig vom einem Lord und seinen Jägern entdeckt wird. Der Lord beschließt, dem Schlafenden einen Streich zu spielen und nimmt Sly mit auf sein Landgut, wo er ihn in ein feudales Schlafzimmer unterbringt. Als Sly erwacht, versuchen der Lord und seine Diener ihn zu überzeugen, dass er selbst Adliger ist, und dass sein Leben als Christopher Sly nur erträumt sei.

Der verwirrte Sly erkennt, dass ihm ein Streich gespielt wird, als er hört wie seine Gläubiger das Haus betreten. Er bittet um eine Minute für sich, währenddessen ergreift er alles Wertvolle und verschwindet aus dem Fenster und singt dabei triumphierend und schadenfroh seine Arie.

THE MASQUE OF ANGELS
„Metatron's Sermon"

In *The Masque of Angels*, eine Kammeroper in einem Akt, wird eine Versammlung mehrerer Engel geschildert, die außerhalb der irdischen Zeitauffassung existieren und deren Aufgabe es ist, Liebe zwischen Sterblichen zu wecken. Die Engel, unter ihnen Chorsänger, Musiker und Tänzer, treffen sich in einer gegenwärtigen Kirche und erwarten ihren Führer, Metatron. Bei seinem Eintreffen verkündet Metatron seinen Engeln den Zweck der Versammlung, nämlich „eine Liebe unter Sterblichen zu ermuntern". Ziel der Arbeit sind ein junger Mann und eine junge Frau, die sich in einer Kirche getroffen haben, sich aber ihrer gegenseitigen Liebe noch nicht sicher sind. Die Engel, die ihnen gegenüber unsichtbar sind, ermutigen sie mit ihren Liedern und Tänzen. Jedoch kommt ihre Botschaft nicht an bis schließlich Metatron das junge Paar in seiner „Sermon" anspricht. Obwohl sie ihn nicht wahrnehmen können, nehmen sie seine Worte auf und sprechen seinen letzten Gedanken selbst aus: „Freude herrscht in der Gegenwart Gottes Engel."

THE SHOEMAKERS' HOLIDAY
„Simon's Aria"
„Ralph's Letter-Ballad"

The Shoemakers' Holiday ist eine Adaptation des gleichnamigen Theaterstücks, das Thomas Dekker um ca. 1600 in London schrieb. Das Stück ist eine Verherrlichung von Tugend und Glück und erzählt die Geschichte des Simon Eyre, dem Schuster des Londoner Oberbürgermeisters. Rowland Lacy, der Neffe des Grafen von Lincoln ist in Rose, der Tochter des Londoner Oberbürgermeisters, verliebt. Weder der Graf noch der Bürgermeister stimmen einer Heirat zu, und beide klügeln einen Plan aus, um die beiden Verliebten zu trennen. Lacy wird ins Ausland abkommandiert, um für das Heer zu kämpfen. Er desertiert und kommt als Holländer verstellt zurück nach London und findet bei Eyre Arbeit. Als Simon Eyre zum Bürgermeister aufsteigt, bekommt er den Segen des Königs für die geplante Heirat zwischen Lacy und Rose.

Bei seinem Aufstieg zum Oberbürgermeister singt Simon seine Arie, die gleichzeitig seine Begeisterung aber auch seine Einsicht zum Ausdruck bringt, das nicht Vernunft sondern ein verrücktes Los ihm diese Leistung gebracht hat.

Gleichzeitig verfolgt das Stück in einer Nebenhandlung Ralph Damport, der als Schuster für Simon arbeitet und seine junge Frau verlassen muss, als er in das Heer einberufen wird. Verwundet und einsam schreibt er Jane eine Brief-Ballade, in der er zuerst seine Trauer beschreibt und dann die Treue seiner Frau erbittet. Seine Sorgen stellen sich als Vorherwissen heraus, denn Jane glaubt, dass er gefallen ist und zieht in einen anderen Stadtteil, wo sie sich von einem skrupellosen Herren hofieren lässt. Im gleichen Sinne der restlichen Oper, kann Ralph seine Frau vor der anstehenden Hochzeit zurückgewinnen. Natürlich ist ihm das Glück dabei hold.

A WATER BIRD TALK
„The Lecturer"

Dominick Argentos *A Water Bird Talk*, eine freie Bearbeitung des „On the Harmfulness of Tobacco" von Chekhov und des „The Birds of America" von Audubon, ist ein mit Humor und Pathos bespicktes Monodrama in einem Akt. Ein Herr mittleren Alters gibt im späten 19. Jahrhundert einen Vortrag über Wasservögel. Die Oper wird gesungen als ob sie an das Publikum des Vortragenden gerichtet ist. Während er die Eigenarten verschiedener Vögel vor einer Diaprojektion von Audubons Zeichnungen beschreibt, macht er unbewusst Vergleiche mit seinem eigenen Leben. Die Jungen des Komorans verlassen nie ihr Nest; das männliche Thorshühnchen kümmert sich um das Häusliche während das Weiblein herumflitzt. Schließlich bekennt er sich als unglücklicher Mensch, der von seiner Frau dominiert und von seinen Töchtern ausgelacht wird. Der Anfang seines Vortrages, der in der Arie „The Lecturer" enthalten ist, zeigt sofort seine Nervosität und seine ängstliche Ehrerbietung gegenüber seiner Frau, die gefühlskalt am Rande sitzt.

JACK BEESON

DR. HEIDEGGER'S FOUNTAIN OF YOUTH
„Prescription for Living"

Dr. Heidegger's Fountain of Youth ist eine Kammeroper in einem Akt nach einer Kurzgeschichte von Nathaniel Hawthorne und bietet eine moralische Lehre anhand einer phantastischen Geschichte, die im Amerika des 19. Jahrhunderts spielt. Der bejahrte Dr. Heidegger lädt vier ebenfalls sehr alte Freunde zu sich ein, um an einem Experiment teilzunehmen. Er hat eine Flasche mit Wasser, das angeblich vom Jungbrunnen geschöpft wurde, und lässt seine Gäste davon trinken. Sie erlangen sehr schnell wieder ihre Jugend, aber zugleich auch ihre jugendliche Leidenschaft. Bald streiten die zwei Damen und zwei Herren um ihre gegenseitige Gunst und zerbrechen dabei die Flasche. Als das Wasser ausläuft, sehen die Gäste entsetzt und traurig wie sie wieder altern. Dr. Heideggers „Prescription for Living" ist die Lehre seines Experiments. Er wird sich mit seinem Alter und seiner Weisheit zufriedengeben. Seine Gäste schenken ihm jedoch wenig Achtung und beschließen den Jungbrunnen selbst zu finden.

HELLO OUT THERE
„The Gambler's Song"

Jack Beesons Kammeroper in einem Akt *Hello Out There* spielt sich innerhalb eines Gefängnisses einer texanischen Kleinstadt ab. Sie beschreibt eine Romanze, die schnell aufblüht und nur Stunden später tragisch endet. Ein junger Mann wacht in Matador Texas hinter Gittern auf, nachdem er im Nachbarsdorf Wheeling zu Unrecht einer Vergewaltigung beschuldigt und verprügelt wurde. Die einzige andere Person, die sich dort befindet ist eine junge Frau, die Gefängnisköchin. Beide fühlen sich zueinander hingezogen und erzählen von ihrer Einsamkeit. Der Spieler verspricht, dass er sie mit nach San Francisco nimmt. In dem Lied „The Gambler's Song" besingt er hoffnungsvoll diese gemeinsame Zukunft.

Besorgt, dass die Männer aus Wheeling ihn finden und umbringen, bittet er die junge Frau ihm eine Schusswaffe zu bringen. Während sie weg ist, finden ihn die Männer auf und erschiessen ihn. Als sie zurückkehrt, liegt er im Sterben und die junge Frau versinkt wieder in Einsamkeit.

LEONARD BERNSTEIN

MASS
„A Simple Song"

Leonard Bernsteins *Mass* (1971) basiert auf der römisch-katholischen Messe, aus der Sicht eines Zelebranten, der gerade in einer Glaubenskrise steckt. Das Stück hält sich genau an die Liturgie, jedoch werden wie in einer Debatte die liturgischen Passagen den häufigen Unterbrechungen und Kommentaren des Zelebranten gegenübergestellt. Der Glaube des Zelebranten ist anfangs unkompliziert und rein, wie es in seinem Wunsch „A Simple Song" als Gotteslob zu singen zum Ausdruck gebracht wird. Jedoch wird sein Glaube unter dem Gewicht des menschlichen Leidens, der Verdorbenheit und den Zeichen der Macht bald untragbar. Am Ende entdeckt der Zelebrant, der kurz davor steht seinen Glauben abzuschwören, dass die Einsamkeit seiner Zweifel schwächer ist als die gemeinsame Freude mit Glaubensgenossen Gott zu loben.

TROUBLE IN TAHITI
„There's a law"

Trouble in Tahiti, Leonard Bernsteins Oper in einem Akt nach seinem 1951 geschriebenen Libretto schildert das Leiden und die Einsamkeit im Leben eines Mannes und einer Frau, die nach außen den amerikanischen Traum darstellen. Die Geschichte handelt vom Streit und der Enttäuschung an einem Tag in ihrem Leben, während ein Jazz-Sängertrio die Tugenden des Amerikanischen Vorstadtlebens lobt.

Sam und Dinah sind seit zehn Jahren verheiratet und haben einen neunjährigen Sohn, der am

Nachmittag des Geschehens bei einer Theateraufführung an seiner Schule die Hauptrolle spielen soll. Sam entschließt sich trotz heftigen Streites mit seiner Frau die Aufführung zu versäumen und anstattdessen in seinem Sportklub an einem Handballturnier teilzunehmen. Nachdem er den Pokal gewonnen hat, singt er in der Umkleidekabine seine Arie „There's a law". Sam erklärt, mit hingerissener Großspurigkeit und vorübergehend unbewusst wie er sich von seiner Familie distanziert, dass er einer der Gewinner im Leben ist.

CARLISLE FLOYD

COLD SASSY TREE
„Rucker's Sermon"
„I've known I've loved you"

Carlisle Floyds Oper *Cold Sassy Tree* beruht auf einem Roman von Olive Ann Burns. Die Geschichte handelt von einem sturen und eigenwilligen Ladeninhaber und Großvater names Rucker Lattimore. Schauplatz ist die Stadt Cold Sassy Tree im Staat Georgia um 1900, wo vor Kurzem Lattimores Frau nach einer langen Krankheit in seiner Pflege verstorben ist. Drei Wochen später teilt er seiner zutiefst bestürzten Familie mit, dass er seine Ladenfrau Love Simpson, die halb so alt ist wie er, heiraten wird. Er versichert ihnen, dass es sich um eine zweckbezogene Heirat handelt: sie werde sich um ihn kümmern, dafür vermache er ihr sein Haus und Gut.

Obwohl Ruckers Familie seine Ehe mit Love im Laufe der Zeit zumindest toleriert, sind die anderen Einwohner Cold Sassys offenbar darüber empört. Als Rucker zum ersten Mal seinen Enkel Will mit Love zur Kirche schickt, ist die Kirchengemeinde so offensichtlich feindselig, dass Will und Love sofort wieder gehen. Zuhause beschließt Rucker seine eigene Kirchenpredigt für Love und seinen bewundernden Enkel zu geben. In „Rucker's Sermon" lässt er sich offen über engstirnige religiöse Fanatiker aus und beendet seine Predigt mit seinem Glauben an Gottes Wunsch, dass Mann und Frau ihr Leben zusammen genießen sollten.

Die Zweckehe verläuft weiterhin reibungslos. Nach kurzer Zeit überrascht Rucker seine Frau, indem er ein Spülklosett für sie installieren lässt. Diesen Luxus hatte er zuvor stets abgelehnt. Er ist von Loves Reaktion darüber so angetan, dass er ihr in seiner Arie „I've known I've loved you" seine wahren Gefühle zeigt. Er verrät ihr, dass er sie schon immer geliebt hat, und dass er sie sich als wahre Ehefrau wünscht.

OF MICE AND MEN
„George's Aria"

Of Mice and Men ist Carlisle Floyds Opernbearbeitung nach John Steinbecks Roman-Klassiker aus dem Jahre 1937. Im Norden Kaliforniens während der Wirtschaftskrise der „Großen Depression" ziehen zwei Wanderarbeiter names George Milton und Lennie Small von einer Ranch zur anderen, um zu arbeiten. Lennie ist ein riesiger Kerl, aber geistig nicht ganz in der Lage seine Kraft einzuschätzen. George ist seit Jahren sein treuer Pfleger. Sie träumen davon eines Tages eine eigene Ranch zu besitzen. Der Traum scheitert letzendlich auf tragische Art und Weise aufgrund Lennies unberechenbarer Kraft.

Kurz nachdem die Beiden in einer neuen Schlafbaracke eintreffen, entdeckt George eine Zeitungsanzeige für eine Ranch, die sie sich mit einem Monatslohn leisten könnten. Slim, der erfahrene Vorarbeiter auf der Ranch sieht wie George die Anzeige genau studiert und versucht ihn abzubringen, da er schon oft erlebt hat wie Arbeiter diesen Traum verfolgen und stets enttäuscht werden. George antwortet mit einer stürmischen Arie und besteht fest darauf, dass er und Lennie Besseres in ihrem Leben finden werden als das Wandern und die Einsamkeit.

THE PASSION OF JONATHAN WADE
„Sleep, conscience, sleep"

Schauplatz für Carlisle Floyd's *The Passion of Jonathan Wade* sind die aschernen Trümmern Columbias, South Carolina, am Ende des amerikanischen Bürgerkrieges. Die Tragödie beschreibt einen Mann, dessen Leben von den selben Kräften zerrissen wird, die nun einen langsamen Wiederaufbau des Südens verhindern könnten. Jonathan Wade, ein Oberst der Armee der Nordstaaten, trifft in Columbia als beaufsichtigender Offizier der Stadt ein. Er hat nicht nur mit den Aufständen der Südstaatenkämpfer zu tun, sondern auch mit den Politikern des Nordens, die diese Situation für sich ausnutzen wollen. Unterdessen verliebt er sich in Celia Townsend, die Tochter eines Richters der Stadt.

Als Jonathan die Anweisung von Washington erhält den Richter Townsend seines Amtes zu entheben, gerät er in einen ernsten Konflikt. Wenn er dem Befehl folgt, wird er Celia und dem ihm gegenüber immer freundlichen und großzügigen Vater im Stich lassen. In „Sleep, conscience, sleep," fleht Jonathan sein Gewissen an, ihn nicht länger wegen der Ausübung seiner Pflicht zu quälen.

SUSANNAH
„Hear me, O Lord"

Carlisle Floyds *Susannah* verkörpert den Süden Amerikas besser als jede andere Oper auf den Bühnen in Amerika und im Ausland. Susannah Polk lebt mit ihrem Bruder Sam in der ruhig gelegenen Gemeinschaft von New Hope Valley in den Bergen von Tennessee mitten im zwanzigsten Jahrhundert. Die Einwohner der Stadt und auch der feurige Pfarrer Olin Blitch, der vor kurzem zur Kirchengemeinde gekommen ist, bezweifeln Susannahs Unschuld aufgrund ihrer jungen Art und ihrer strahlenden Schönheit. Nachdem man sie beim Baden in einem Bach erwischt, wird sie von den Kirchenältesten boshaft beschuldigt eine Ehebrecherin zu sein, und sie wird aus der Gemeinde gestoßen. Pfarrer Blitch besucht Susannah zu Hause, um sie zur Reue zu überreden, aber anstattdessen erliegt er seinem Begehren für das Mädchen, das zu erschöpft ist ihn abzuwehren.

Blitch singt am nächsten Morgen alleine in seiner Kirche sein Gebet der Reue als ihm zu spät klar wird, dass Susannah unschuldig ist und welch schwerwiegende Sünde er begangen hat. Obwohl er seine Intimität mit Susannah nicht zugibt, bittet er die Kirchengemeinde Susannah zu verzeihen, aber die Gemeinde weigert sich an ihre Unschuld zu glauben. Es kommt zu keiner Vergebung, denn Sam, der von der Jagd zurückgekehrt ist, erfährt von Susannahs Geschichte und bringt Blitch in einem Wutanfall um.

WILLIE STARK
„Single bed blanket"
„We all come out of the earth"

Willie Stark ist Carlisle Floyds Adaptation des Robert Penn Warren Romans *All the King's Men*, die den Aufstieg und den Abgang eines mächtigen Gouverneurs im tiefen Süden Amerikas beschreibt. Die Armen auf dem Land verehren Stark wegen seiner populistischen Überzeugung, aber die eingesessene politische Führung verachtet ihn wegen seines unnachgiebigen Handelns. Stark hat in der Politik eine ebenso gigantische Gegenwart wie im Leben der Personen um ihn herum.

Ein heißer Kampf spitzt sich in der Landeshauptstadt zu. Denn Starks Feinde wollen ein Amtsenthebungsverfahren gegen ihn einleiten, weil er angeblich die Gerichte zum Vorteil seiner Sozialreformen beeinflusst hat. Als Stark davon erfährt, dass der hoch angesehene Richter Burden dem Fall für die Amtsenthebung beipflichten will, stattet er ihm mit der Absicht ihn umzustimmen einen Besuch ab. Der Richter antwortet kurz und prägnant, dass er Starks Amtsenthebung wegen seiner „Missachtung des Gesetzes" unterstützen wolle. Stark antwortet mit seiner Arie „Single bed blanket," in der er seine populistische Auffassung des Gesetzes anhand einer volkstümlichen Parabel zu erklären versucht.

Bei einer Kundgebung vor dem Gerichtsgebäude in sejner Heimatstadt Mason City am selben Tag ist Stark plötzlich vom Angesicht eines Jungen mit einer Mundharmonika, der ihn an seine Jugend erinnert, sehr angetan. Er kauft dem Jungen die

Mundharmonika ab und singt „We all come out of the earth". In diesem Moment verliert Stark die Härte des Politikers und sinniert über den Verlauf seines bisherigen Lebens. Ihm wird dabei klar, dass er sich nach dem verlorenen Bild seiner Person sehnt.

DOUGLAS MOORE

THE DEVIL AND DANIEL WEBSTER
„I've got a ram, Goliath"

Das Stück The Devil and Daniel Webster spielt im Staat New Hampshire um 1840 und lässt auf erstklassige Weise den Teufel gegen den genialen Anwalt und Staatsmann antreten. Webster ist der Ehrengast auf der Hochzeit von Jabez Stone, ein Senator des Bundesstaates, dem es auf geheimnisvollem Weg gelang sich aus der Armut zu retten. Die Festlichkeiten werden vom bösen Scratch, der sich später als der Teufel entpuppt, unterbrochen. Jabez gibt zu vor zehn Jahren seine Seele verkauft zu haben. Daraufhin erklärt sich Webster bereit ihn vor Gericht zu vertreten. Scratch sucht sich selbst die Geschworenen aus, die allesamt berüchtigte Verräter sind, die von der Hölle zurückgeholt wurden. Sie schlagen Websters rechtliche Begründungen nieder, jedoch werden auch sie letztendlich von seinem Appell an Leben und Freiheit umgestimmt. Jabez Stone heiratet, und die jubelnden Einheimischen treiben den Teufel aus New Hampshire.

Webster singt in seiner Arie „I've got a ram, Goliath" über seine Kraft als Bauer und seine Entschlossenheit Freiheit zu verteidigen.

NED ROREM

THE ROBBERS
„I cannot still the echo"

Ned Rorems The Robbers ist eine Kammeroper in einer Szene nach Pardoner's Tale aus Chaucers Canterbury Tales. Drei Wegelagerer haben einen Fremden auf ein Zimmer in einem Gasthaus gelockt, ihm seines Goldes beraubt und ihn umgebracht. Der junge und unerfahrene Räuber ist von dem Mord erschüttert. Aus Gier und aus Angst von ihm verraten zu werden planen die zwei anderen Räuber den Neuling in der Nacht umzubringen.

Währenddessen grübelt der Neuling über den Mord. In seiner Arie „I cannot still the echo" weichen seine Bedenken der bösen Absicht die anderen zwei umzubringen, damit er das ganze Gold für sich hat.

Der Neuling vergiftet eine Flasche Wein und bringt sie den anderen zwei Räubern, die ihn umbringen und anschließend den Wein trinken. Der Vorhang fällt auf vier Leichen und einen verstreuten Haufen Gold.

IGOR STRAVINSKY

THE RAKE'S PROGRESS
„Nick Shadow's Aria"

Strawinsky schrieb 1951 seine geniale neoklassische Oper The Rake's Progress als er in Hollywood lebte. W.H. Audens Libretto beschreibt die Geschichte Tom Rakewells, ein müßiggängerischer junger Mann, der sein Leben lieber vom Glück als vom Verdienst leiten lässt. Als der böse Nick Shadow ihm von einer Erbschaft eines unbekannten Onkels erzählt, geht Tom mit Nick nach London. Er beabsichtigt seine Geschäfte zu erledigen und dann sein Liebling Anne Trulove zu holen. Anstattdessen, verleitet Shadow den schwachen Tom auf selbstzerstörerischer Art jegliche Tugendhaftigkeit in den Wind zu werfen.

Tom ist nach kurzer Zeit in London unglücklich und unzufrieden. Shadow macht ihm den unglaublichen Vorschlag die europaweit bekannte bärtige Türkin, Baba the Turk, zu heiraten. Tom reagiert zunächst zweifelnd, aber schließlich überzeugt ihn Nick mit seiner verschlagenen Arie. Er erklärt, dass Männer unglücklich sind, weil sie nicht frei sind. Und um frei zu sein, müssen sie Verlangen und Verstand ablegen.

JOHN ADAMS

I WAS LOOKING AT THE CEILING AND THEN I SAW THE SKY
«Dewain's Song of Liberation and Surprise»

I Was Looking at the Ceiling and Then I Saw the Sky es una singular «obra cantada» en dos actos que compuso Adams en 1995 con un libreto del poeta June Jordan. *Ceiling/Sky*, un romance, comedia y sátira social mordaz, presenta las vidas de siete hombres y mujeres jóvenes que viven en un vecindario pobre de Los Angeles, donde luchan contra las dificultades y paradojas de sus vidas cotidianas. Un fuerte terremoto asola la ciudad, poniendo sus conflictos y amores en mayor relieve—pero inspirando a la vez claridad e incluso consuelo.

En el momento del terremoto, Dewain está en la cárcel, enfrentando un juicio por un delito menor que, no obstante, puede dejarlo encarcelado la mayor parte de su vida si lo condenan. Cantando desde las ruinas de su celda, la cual ha sido destruida por el terremoto, «Dewain's Song of Liberation and Surprise» expresa el impacto de la libertad literal y repentina, la cual se ve transcendida en sí por la revelación de su libertad innata.

EL NIÑO
«Dawn Air»
«Shake the heavens»

El Niño (2000) cuenta la historia de la Navidad, basando su texto en una variedad de fuentes: Evangelios del Nuevo Testamento, profesías del Viejo Testamento, episodios casi desconocidos de textos apócrifos, y poesía mexicana del sigloXX (en español e inglés) que imparten una resonancia contemporánea a la ópera/oratorio.

«Dawn Air», escrita por Vicente Huidobro (1893–1948) y adaptada aquí en una traducción de David Guss, invoca imágenes majestuosas y naturales para transmitir una canción de amor y elogio. «Shake the heavens» toma como texto tres versículos del libro de Haggai del Viejo Testamento. Estas palabras de Dios, una promesa de remecer los cielos, la tierra y el mar, dan miedo pero en definitiva celebran el poder de Dios para traer gloria y paz en la tierra.

NIXON IN CHINA
«News Aria»
«Chou En-lai's Epilogue»

La opera *Nixon in China* que compuso John Adams en 1987 se ha hecho famosa por su tema innovador. La reunión del Presidente Richard Nixon en 1973 con el Presidente Mao Tse-Tung de China fue un acontecimiento dramático en sí, señalando un compromiso nuevo y precavido entre naciones poderosas. La libretista de *Nixon in China*, Alice Goodman, presenta a Nixon, Mao, sus colaboradores y sus esposas como personas complejas que se encuentran en circunstancias heroicas. Los ojos del mundo convergen en ellos, pero ellos no pueden expresar los sueños, las angustias ni los recuerdos que hacen surgir estos sucesos de la época.

Nixon canta su primera aria en la ópera, «News has a kind of mystery», después de bajar de su avión Air Force One y encontrarse con el Primer Ministro chino, Chou En-lai. Con un aire nervioso de idealismo entusiasta, el Presidente describe su deleite al imaginarse en el umbral de la historia. Pero poco despues, pasa a meditar sobre las aprensiones y el peso de su próxima tarea.

El tercer acto de la ópera se desarrolla durante la última noche de la visita, y encuentra a todos los personajes fatigados e introspectivos. El «Epilogue» de Chou En-lai concluye la ópera con una tranquila reflexión sobre la vejez, el remordimiento, el arrepentimiento y las limitaciones de las acciones humanas.

DOMINICK ARGENTO

THE BOOR
«The Boor's Aria»

La ópera buffa en un solo acto, *The Boor*, de Dominick Argento trata acerca de la obra homóloga de Anton Chekhov. Un año después de morir su esposo, una viuda todavía lo llora constantemente, a pesar de que solía dejarla días enteros para ir a ver a sus amantes. Repentinamente in hombre irrumpe en su casa de campo y le exige que le pague inmediatamente una deuda que dejó su esposo, para poder pagar un préstamo del banco al día siguiente. Pero la viuda no puede darle el dinero hasta el día siguiente, y se niega a pensar más en el asunto debido a su «estado mental» en el aniversario de la muerte de su esposo. Ella sale abruptamente de la sala y el patán canta su aria indignada: se le acusa constantemente de ser un patán, pero realmente es otra gente la que siempre lo trata mal a él.

Por último la viuda y el patán resuelven batirse a duelo. Pero cuando están preparando sus pistolas, el patán se enamora de la fortaleza y carácter de la viuda. En vez de dar un tiro, el duelo termina en un beso y, finalmente, la viuda se siente lista para volver a disfrutar de la vida sin afliciones.

CASANOVA'S HOMECOMING
«Casanova's Final Air»

Las hazañas de Giacomo Casanova—el viajero veneciano del siglo XVIII, académico, estafador, escritor, diplomático, jugador, empresario, músico y amante insaciable por añadidura—podría protagonizar varias óperas cómicas. *Casanova's Homecoming* de Argento trata acerca de un par de episodios seleccionados ambientados en 1774, cuando Casanova regresa a Venecia después de veinte año de exilio. Para proveer la dote para Barbara, la hija de una ex-amante, Casanova explota la riqueza de una viuda acomodada que cree en sus supuestos poderes paranormales con el más allá. Con la ayuda de sus amigos, él tiene éxito en su fraude mientras evade astutamente a las autoridades de la ciudad, quienes sospechan que sigue haciendo de las suyas.

Después de la boda de Barbara, Casanova dirige a los presentes en un brindis por los novios y luego canta su «Final Air», la cual resume el credo de su vida, y de la ópera: vivir, amar y amar vivir.

CHRISTOPHER SLY
«Sly's Aria»

La historia de Christopher Sly, que sirve como introducción de *The Taming of the Shrew* de Shakespeare, es independiente en la ópera de cámara en un acto de Argento. Sly ha caído en un sopor ebrio a la salida de una taberna mientras huía de sus acreedores, y se lo encuentra un Lord y su séquito de caza. El Lord decide jugarle una broma a Sly, llevándolo a su finca y acomodándolo en unos aposentos lujosos. Cuando Sly despierta, el Lord y sus sirvientes procuran convencerlo de que realmente es un lord, y que su vida como Christopher Sly fue sólo un sueño.

El aturdido Sly se da cuenta de que le han jugado una mala pasada cuando escucha que sus acreedores entran a la finca. Pidiendo un minuto de soledad, se apodera de todo lo valioso que tiene a mano y se fuga por la ventana, cantando al mismo tiempo su aria triunfal y resentida.

THE MASQUE OF ANGELS
«Metatron's Sermon»

La ópera de cámara en un acto *The Masque of Angels* presenta una reunión de ángeles, quienes existen fuera de la percepción terrenal del tiempo pero se dedican a la causa de inspirar amor entre los mortales. Con coristas, músicos y bailarines en sus filas, los ángeles se reúnen en una iglesia de la era actual y esperan a su líder, Metatron. Al llegar, Metatron informa a los ángeles el objetivo de su reunión: «fomentar un amor mortal.» Una pareja de jóvenes están desplegando sus esfuerzos; se han encontrado en la iglesia, inseguros de su amor mutuo. Los ángeles, invisibles para ellos, los van alentando a través de canciones y danzas, pero su mensaje todavía elude a la joven pareja. Finalmente, Metatron les entrega su «Sermon»; aunque no pueden percibir su presencia, los amantes absorben sus palabras y se repiten a sí mismos su última frase: «Hay alegría en la compañía de los ángeles de Dios.»

THE SHOEMAKERS' HOLIDAY
«Simon's Aria»
«Ralph's Letter-Ballad»

The Shoemakers' Holiday es una adaptación de la obra homónima de Thomas Dekker, escrita en Londres alrededor de 1600. Una celebración de mucho espíritu de la virtud y la buena fortuna, la historia se centra alrededor de la tienda de Simon Eyre, el zapatero del Alcalde de Londres. Rowland Lacy, sobrino del Conde de Lincoln, está enamorado de Rose, hija del Alcalde. Pero ni el Conde ni el Alcalde desean que ambos se casen, así es que se confabulan para separar a los amantes. Lacy es enviado al extranjero a combatir en el ejército, pero deserta y regresa a Londres disfrazado de holandés, y trabaja en la tienda de Eyre. Simon Eyre asciende hasta convertirse en Alcalde él mismo y, en calidad de tal, se asegura la bendición del Rey para casar a Lacy y Rose.

Simon canta su aria al asumir como Alcalde y baila con entusiasmo y reconocimiento de que la loca fortuna, y no la razón, ha facilitado su logro.

Entre tanto, una trama secundaria se desenvuelve con Ralph Damport, uno de los zapateros de Simon, quien es reclutado por el ejército y separado de su joven esposa, Jane. Herido y solitario, Ralph escribe a Jane en una «Letter-Ballad», en la cual su tristeza gradualmente desemboca en un ruego para que tenga paciencia. Las preocupaciones de Ralph son proféticas, porque Jane, creyéndolo muerto, se traslada a otra parte de Londres y permite que la corteje un caballero inescrupuloso de la ciudad. Pero manteniendo el espíritu del resto de la ópera, Ralph logra recuperarla casi a punto de casarse—claro que no sin la ayuda de la buena fortuna.

A WATER BIRD TALK
«The Lecturer»

A Water Bird Talk, adaptada libremente por Dominick Argento de la obra de Chekhov «On the Harmfulness of Tobacco» y «The Birds of America», de Audubon es un monodrama de un acto con toques de humor y aflicción. A fines del siglo XIX, un caballero de mediana edad da una conferencia sobre las aves acuáticas; la ópera se canta como si se dirigiera a la audiencia del conferencista. Al describir los hábitos de diversas aves, frente a las diapositivas proyectadas de las ilustraciones de Audubon, sin darse cuenta traza paralelos con su propia vida. Las crías del cormorán nunca dejan el nido; el macho falaropo se encarga de las labores domésticas mientras la hembra revolotea por ahí. Por último se revela como un hombre desdichado, hostigado por su esposa y burlado por sus hijas.

El comienzo de su discurso, incluido en el aria «The Lecturer», inmediatamente demuestra su nerviosidad y tímida deferencia hacia su esposa, quien aparece sentada hostilmente al costado.

JACK BEESON

DR. HEIDEGGER'S FOUNTAIN OF YOUTH
«Prescription for Living»

Dr. Heidegger's Fountain of Youth, una ópera de cámara en un solo acto adaptada de un cuento corto de Nathaniel Hawthorne, presenta una lección moral a través de una historia fantástica ambientada en los Estados Unidos del siglo XIX. El viejo Dr. Heidegger invita a cuatro amigos, todos ancianos también, a su casa para participar en un experimento. Presenta un frasco de agua supuestamente tomada de la legendaria Fuente de la Juventud y cada uno de sus invitados bebe un sorbo. Rápidamente comienzan a recobrar su juventud, pero también vuelven sus pasiones juveniles. Las dos mujeres y los dos hombres pronto se encuentran peleando por las atenciones mutuas, y en el barullo se vuelca y rompe el frasco. Al volcarse el agua, vuelve la vejez a los invitados sorprendidos y entristecidos de Heidegger.

«Prescription for Living» del Dr. Heidegger es su lección del experimento: está satisfecho con su ancianidad y sabiduría. Pero sus amigos no prestan atención alguna, y juran buscar la Fuente de la Juventud ellos mismos.

HELLO OUT THERE
«The Gambler's Song»

Desarrollándose totalmente dentro de los confines de la cárcel de un pequeño pueblo en Tejas, la ópera de cámara de Jack Beeson en un acto *Hello Out There* retrata un romance que florece rápidamente, para terminar después en una tragedia terrible horas más tarde. Un joven despierta tras las rejas en Matador, Tejas, habiendo sido acusado falsamente de violación y luego golpeado en Wheeling, un pueblo cercano. La única otra persona cercana es una joven, la cocinera de la cárcel, y los dos se sienten rápidamente atraídos. Cada cual revela su soledad, y el jugador dice a la joven que se la llevará a San Francisco con él. En «The Gambler's Song», él canta esperanzado sobre ese futuro.

Temeroso de que los hombres de Wheeling lo vayan a encontrar y lo maten, el jugador envía a la joven a buscar un fusil. Mientras ella está fuera, los hombres llegan y lo acribillan. La joven regresa y él muere, y ella se repliega nuevamente en su soledad.

LEONARD BERNSTEIN

MASS
«A Simple Song»

La *Mass* (1971) de Leonard Bernstein se basa en la misa católica romana, vista desde la perspectiva de un sacerdote que vive una crisis de fe. Sigue la liturgia exactamente, pero los pasajes litúrgicos se yuxtaponen contra interrupciones y comentarios frecuentes del sacerdote y de la congregación, de manera muy similar a un debate en curso.

La fe del sacerdote es al principio simple y pura, como lo demuestra su deseo de cantar «A Simple Song» en tributo a Dios. Pero esa fe gradualmente pasa a hacerse insostenible bajo el peso de la miseria humana, la corrupción y las antimañas del poder humano. Al final, el sacerdote, a punto de renunciar a su fe, encuentra que la soledad de su duda no se compara con la alegría de reunirse con otros creyentes en el culto.

TROUBLE IN TAHITI
«There's a law»

La ópera en un solo acto de Leonard Bernstein *Trouble in Tahiti*, escrita con su propio libreto en 1951, presenta la angustia y la soledad en las vidas de un matrimonio que aparentan vivir el sueño americano. La trama sigue las discusiones y las frustraciones de un solo día de su vida, mientras un trío de cantantes de jazz elogia las virtudes de la vida familiar en los suburbios.

Sam ha estado casado con Dinah casi diez años, y tienen un hijo de nueve años, quien esta tarde está jugando el rol principal en una obra teatral en su escuela. Sam, a pesar de las discusiones de Dinah con él, insiste en no ir a la presentación y jugar, en cambio, un torneo de balonmano en su gimnasio. Después en los vestidores, habiendo ganado el trofeo de balonmano, Sam canta su aria «There's a law». Con una arrogancia extasiada y temporalmente inconsciente de la manera en que se está distanciando de su familia, Sam declara que es uno de los ganadores de la vida.

CARLISLE FLOYD

COLD SASSY TREE
«Rucker's Sermon»
«I've known I've loved you»

La ópera de Carlisle Floyd *Cold Sassy Tree*, basada en la novela de Olive Ann Burns, se centra en Rucker Lattimore, dueño de una tienda y abuelo con sus idiosincrasias obstinadas. En el pueblo de Cold Sassy Tree, Georgia, en 1900, Lattimore hace poco ha visto morir a su esposa después de una larga agonía. Sorprende a su familia tres semanas después al anunciar su matrimonio con Love Simpson, empleada de su tienda que tiene la mitad de su edad. Tranquilizándolos, les explica que se trata solamente de un «matrimonio de nombre»—ella lo cuidará y, a cambio, le legará su casa y sus muebles por testamento.

Aunque la familia de Rucker llega a tolerar este matrimonio con Love, apenas, los demás residentes de Cold Sassy Tree demuestran abiertamente su disgusto con la situación. Cuando Rucker envía a su nieto, Will, a la iglesia con Love por primera vez, los feligreses les son abiertamente hostiles; Love y Will se van inmediatamente. De vuelta en casa, Rucker decide realizar su propia misa, sólo para Love y su nieto que lo admira. «Rucker's Sermon» expresa abiertamente sus creencias acerca de los fanáticos religiosos intolerantes, y concluye con una afirmación del deseo de Dios de que hombres y mujeres valoren y disfruten de sus vidas.

El matrimonio sólo de nombre continúa armoniosamente, y después de un tiempo Rucker incluso sorprende a Love al instalar un sistema de plomería en la casa—un gasto que obstinadamente siempre se había rehusado a hacer. Emocionado por la reacción de felicidad de Love, Rucker finalmente admite lo que siente por ella: en su aria «I've known I've loved you» le confiesa que la ha amado desde el principio y que desea que sea verdaderamente su esposa.

OF MICE AND MEN
«George's Aria»

Of Mice and Men es la adaptación operática de Carlisle Floyd de la novela clásica de John Steinbeck que data de 1937. En el norte de California en la era de la Gran Depresión, dos trabajadores migratorios, George Milton y Lennie Small, vagan de un trabajo a otro en distintos ranchos. Lennie es un hombre enorme, pero de poco seso para darse cuenta de su fuerza; George es su cuidador leal de toda la vida. Su único sueño es algún día ser dueños de un rancho juntos, pero a fin de cuentas no se hace realidad porque la fuerza peligrosa de Lennie desemboca en tragedia.

Poco después de llegar los dos a una nueva barraca de obreros, George descubre un anuncio en el periódico sobre un rancho en venta suficientemente barato para que los dos puedan pagarlo con un mes de trabajo. El experimentado capataz del rancho, Slim, observa a George leyendo el anuncio y trata de disuadirlo para que no crea en ese sueño, donde ha visto caer ya a muchos obreros, resultando sólo en una amarga desilusión. George responde con un aria vehemente, en la cual insiste que él y Lennie encontrarán algo más en sus vidas que la vagancia y la soledad.

THE PASSION OF JONATHAN WADE
«Sleep, conscience, sleep»

Ambientada en la ruina ennegrecida de Columbia, Carolina del Sur, al terminar la Guerra Civil, *The Passion of Jonathan Wade* de Carlisle Floyd es la tragedia de la vida de un hombre dividido entre las mismas fuerzas que amenazan la problemática reconstrucción del Sur. Jonathan Wade, coronel del ejército de la Unión, llega a Columbia como oficial a cargo de supervisar la ciudad. Por un lado, lucha con rebeldes intransigentes dedicados a la violencia; y por el otro, con políticos del Norte que explotan la situación para su propia conveniencia política. Mientras tanto, él se enamora de Celia Townsend, hija de un juez local.

Cuando Washington de dice a Jonathan que destituya al Juez Townsend de su cargo, él se siente particularmente desgarrado. Si obedece la orden, traiciona a Celia, así como al Juez mismo, que ha sido hospitalario y generoso hacia él. En «Sleep, conscience, sleep» Jonathan implora a su conciencia que lo deje de atormentar con el deber que debe cumplir.

SUSANNAH
«Hear me, O Lord»

Susannah, de Carlisle Floyd, más que ninguna otra ópera, ha llegado a representar el Sur de los Estados Unidos en los escenarios de ese país y del extranjero. En las montañas de Tennessee, a mediados del siglo XX, Susannah Polk vive con su hermano Sam en la comunidad apartada de New Hope Valley. La juventud y la belleza radiante de Susannah hacen que la gente que la circunda—incluido el furibundo Reverendo Olin Blitch, recién llegado a la iglesia local—desconfíe de su inocencia. Después de haberla espiado bañándose en un arroyo, las autoridades eclesiásticas la acusan cruelmente de ser una adúltera malvada, y la convierten en una paria de la comunidad. El Reverendo Blitch va a la casa de Susannah para presionarla para que se arrepienta, pero en vez de hacerlo consuma su propio deseo por la joven, quien está demasiado exhausta para resistirse.

Blitch canta su Oración de arrepentimiento a la mañana siguiente, solo en su iglesia, al darse cuenta tardíamente de la inocencia de Susannah y del peso de su propio pecado. Cuando llegan sus feligreses, él les ruega que pidan a Susannah que los perdone—aunque no admite su intimidad con ella—pero ellos se niegan a creer en su inocencia. El perdón no se logra dado que Sam, al regresar de una expedición de caza, escucha el relato de Susannah y mata a Blitch en un arranque de ira.

WILLIE STARK
«Single bed blanket»
«We all come out of the earth»

Willie Stark es la adaptación hecha por Carlisle Floyd de la novela de Robert Penn Warren titulada *All the King's Men*, la cual cuenta del auge y caída de un poderoso gobernador sureño. Stark cuenta con simpatías entre los pobres de las zonas rurales por sus convicciones populistas, pero es detestado por la maquinaria política estatal por sus maniobras brutales. La magnitud política titánica de Stark es igualada por la presencia abrumadora que impone su personalidad en las vidas de quienes lo rodean.

Una batalla acalorada tiene lugar en el capitolio estatal, mientras los enemigos políticos de Stark luchan por comenzar un proceso de denuncia en su contra, basándose en la manipulación que ha hecho Stark del sistema judicial estatal en pro de sus reformas sociales. Cuando Stark escucha que el Juez Burden, altamente respetado, se está preparando para aprobar el caso de denuncia, lo visita en su casa para disuadirlo. La respuesta del Juez es breve pero incisiva: apoyará la denuncia porque Stark «no respeta la ley». Stark responde con el aria «Single bed blanket» demostrando su propia visión populista de la ley en la forma de una sencilla parábola.

Más tarde en el mismo día, durante una demostración en los peldaños de los tribunales de su pueblo natal, Mason City, Stark se conmueve repentinamente al ver a un niño con una armónica entre la multitud. Recordando su propia juventud, Stark le compra la armónica al niño y canta «We all come out of the earth». Perdiendo su habitual dureza de político, Stark rememora la trayectoria de su vida y se da cuenta de que extraña la visión de sí mismo que ha dejado atrás.

DOUGLAS MOORE

THE DEVIL AND DANIEL WEBSTER
«I've got a ram, Goliath»

The Devil and Daniel Webster, ambientada en New Hampshire en la década de 1840, estupendamente enfrenta al Demonio contra el brillante abogado y estadista estadounidense. Webster es el invitado de honor en el matrimonio de Jabez Stone, un senador del estado que se las había ingeniado misteriosamente para surgir de una persistente pobreza. Las festividades se ven interrumpidas por el siniestro Scratch, quien tiempo después se desenmascara como el Demonio. Jabez admite que vendió su alma hace diez años, pero Webster ofrece defender su caso. El jurado especialmente seleccionado de Scratch, compuesto por traidores infames traídos del infierno, obstruye los argumentos legales de Webster, pero incluso ellos se convencen con su apelación final a la vida y a la libertad. Jabez Stone se casa, y los vecinos jubilosos destierran al Demonio de New Hampshire.

En su aria «I've got a ram, Goliath» Webster canta sobre su fortaleza como granjero y su determinación para defender la libertad.

NED ROREM

THE ROBBERS
«I cannot still the echo»

The Robbers de Ned Rorem es una ópera de cámara en una sola escena, adaptada del *Pardoner's Tale*, entre los *Canterbury Tales* de Chaucer. Tres matones han atraído a un extraño a un cuarto de una hospedería, donde lo asesinan por su oro. Uno de los ladrones es joven y sin experiencia, y queda impresionado por el asesinato. Los otros dos, motivados por la avaricia y también preocupados por el novato que puede delatar inadvertidamente el crimen, confabulan para matarlo más tarde esa noche.

Mientras tanto, el novato continúa su remordimiento por el asesinato. En su aria «I cannot still the echo» sus inquietudes se mezclan gradualmente con una idea siniestra: si mata a los otros dos, todo el oro será suyo.

El novato envenena una botella de vino, y se la lleva a sus compañeros. Ellos lo matan y después beben, cerrándose posteriormente el telón sobre los cuatro cadáveres y una pila de oro desparramado.

IGOR STRAVINSKY

THE RAKE'S PROGRESS
«Nick Shadow's Aria»

Igor Stravinsky escribió su brillante ópera neoclásica *The Rake's Progress* en 1951 cuando vivía en Hollywood. El libreto de W.H. Auden cuenta la historia de Tom Rakewell, un joven ocioso que resuelve dejar que la fortuna guíe su destino, en vez del mérito. Cuando el siniestro Nick Shadow llega con la noticia de una herencia de un tío desconocido, Tom parte con él a Londres, para encargarse de sus asuntos y luego mandar a buscar a su amada Anne Trulove. Contrariamente a lo planeado, el carácter débil de Tom lo hace fácil presa de Shadow, quien lo guía a abandonar autodestructivamente toda virtud.

Después de poco tiempo en Londres, Tom se siente insatisfecho y descontento. Shadow le hace una propuesta descabellada: Tom debe casarse con Baba la Turca, una dama barbuda famosa en toda Europa. Tom reacciona incrédulo, pero Shadow lo convence del plan con un aria engañosa: los hombres son infelices porque no son libres, y para ser libres, deben abandonar tanto la razón como el deseo.

アダムズ、「私は天井を眺めて、それから空を見た」:ディウェインの「解放と驚きの歌」

　「天井を眺めて、それから空を見た」は、詩人ジューン・ジョーダンの歌詞に付けるために、1995年にアダムズが独自に執筆した第2幕の「歌劇」です。「天井・空」は、ロマンス、コメディ、痛烈な社会風刺で、日常生活の苦難と矛盾と格闘しながら、ロサンジェルスの貧民地区に住んでいる7人の若い男女を歌っています。大地震がロサンジェルスを襲い、軋轢と愛情が急速に揺らぐが、明るさと安らぎも感じられます。
地震のときにドウェインは刑務所におり、些細な罪で裁判にかけられています。もし有罪となれば、ほぼ全人生を刑務所で過ごすことになるでしょう。地震で崩壊した独房の廃墟から歌う「ディウェインの解放と驚きの歌」は、突然のショックと文字通りの自由を歌い上げます。生まれながらに与えられているはずの自由が、天啓として超越的に告げられています。

アダムズ、エル・ニーニョ「暁の旋律」:天界を揺らせ。

　エル・ニーニョ(2000)はキリスト生誕の物語を述べており、その内容は様々な出典から取られています：新約聖書の福音、旧約聖書の予言、真偽の疑わしい文書の風変わりなエピソード およびオペラへの現代的共鳴を与える20世紀のメキシコの詩（スペイン語と英語の両方で）。
　ビンセンテ・ウィドブロ(1893-1948)の「暁の旋律」については、デイヴィッド・ガスの翻訳版を掲載します。これは壮大なイメージが自然に思い浮かぶ、愛と賞賛の歌です。「天界を揺らせ」は、旧約聖書（ハガイ書）の3つの詩から引用されています。このような神の言葉、天界、地界、海を揺らすという約束は恐ろしいが、最後には神の力を讃え、地界に栄光と平和をもたらすという歌です。

ジョン・アダムズ、「中国のニクソン」:周恩来のエピローグ

　ジョン・アダムズによる1987年のオペラ「中国のニクソン」は、その画期的な主題で有名になりました。リチャード・ニクソン大統領と中国の毛沢東主席との1973年会見は、それ自体が劇的な出来事で、強力な国家間の新しく用心深い交わりの前兆を示すものでした。「中国のニクソン」の台本作者であるアリス・グッドマンは、ニクソンと毛沢東、そして彼らの仲間と配偶者達を、気がつくと英雄的な状況にいることになった通常の人々として描いています。世界中の目が彼らに注がれていますが、それでも彼らは、これらの画期的な出来事にかき立てられた夢や心配や記憶を言葉にして表わさずにいられません。
　ニクソンは、大統領専用機から降り立って中国首相の周恩来と会った後、このオペラのニクソン最初のアリア、「ニュースはちょっとした神秘」を歌います。緊張しつつも理想主義に胸を高鳴らせ、大統領は歴史的出来事の最前線における自分の姿を想像しながら、高揚した気持ちを歌い上げます。しかし、すぐに目前の任務の重荷と不安に思案するようになります。
このオペラの第3幕は、訪中の最後の晩であります。登場人物全員が疲弊して、内省しています。昔の時代、自責の念、悔恨、人間の行動の限界について、静かに瞑想しながら周恩来のエピローグで、オペラは幕を閉じます。

アルジェント、「田舎者」*田舎者のアリア*

　　　ドミニク・アルジェントの一幕喜歌劇*「田舎者」*は、アントン・チェホフの同名劇を扱ったものです。夫が死んで１年後、生前彼が浮気相手に会うために続けて何日も他所に泊まっていたにもかかわらず、未亡人は依然として彼をしのんで嘆き悲しみ続けています。田舎にある彼女の邸宅に突然一人の男が無理やり押しかけて来て、彼女の夫が残した借金を払うよう要求します。そうすれば男は翌日、銀行ローンを返済できるからです。未亡人は翌日まで男に返済できないが、その日が夫の１周忌であるという「精神状態」のために、この問題をそれ以上考えないようにしています。未亡人は無愛想に部屋を去り、田舎者はアリアを歌います。男はいつも「田舎者」と責められているが、いつも男に失礼な態度を示すのは、周りの人間の方であります。
最後に未亡人と田舎者は、決闘を決意します。ピストルを準備しつつ、田舎者は未亡人の強さと精神力に魅了されていきます。決闘で打ち合いをする代わりにキスをして、とうとう未亡人は嘆かずに、また人生を生きられるようになります。

アルジェント、「カサノヴァの帰省」:*「カサノバの最後の旋律」*

　　　ジャコモ・カサノヴァ（18世紀のベニスの旅行者、学者、詐欺師、記述家、外交官、賭博師、起業家、音楽家、飽くことを知らない恋人）の活躍を盛り込んだ喜歌劇はいくつもあります。アルジェントの*「カサノヴァの帰省」*は、カサノヴァが刑務所から逃げて20年間の流浪の後、1774年にヴェニスへ帰って来ます。以前の恋人の娘に結婚持参金を渡すため、カサノヴァは、彼が持つと思われている超自然的な力を信じている裕福な未亡人から富を引き出します。友人の助けを得て首尾よく詐欺を成し遂げ、彼は、彼がまだ悪事をたくらんでいるのではないかと疑っている市の当局の追求を巧妙に回避します。
　　　カサノヴァはバーバラの結婚式の後、花嫁と花婿への乾杯の音頭を取り、「最後の旋律」を歌います。この歌は、カサノヴァの人生、そして、このオペラの集大成であります。すなわち、「生きる。愛する。生きることを愛する」ということです。

アルジェント、「クリストファー・スライ」:*スライのアリア*

　　　「クリストファー・スライ」の物語（シェークスピアの「じゃじゃ馬ならし」の序文となる）は、アルジェントの一幕室内オペラの中で、それ自体が独立したものです。スライは、債権者から逃れる間に、ビール店の外で酔払って眠り込んでしまいます。そして、彼は狩猟に行った領主の一行によって偶然見つけられます。その領主はスライをからかおうと、自分の領地へ彼を連れて行き、豪華な寝室に寝かせます。スライが目覚めると、領主とその使用人達は、彼が本当に領主であり、クリストファー・スライという彼の生活は単なる夢だったのだと説得しようとします。
　　　債権者が館に来て声が聞こえたときに、自分はひっかけられているのだと、呆然としていたスライは気づきます。ちょっと１人になりたいと願い出て、掴めるだけの貴重品を掴み、意気揚々とアリアを歌いながら窓からそっと出て行きました。

ドミニク・アルジェント、「天使の仮面」：メタトロンの説教

　「天使の仮面」は、1幕オペラで天使の集会を題材にしています。天使は地界の時間感覚とは異なる世界に生きているが、人と人との間の愛を促すという理想に専念しています。部下の聖歌隊、音楽家、踊り手を携え、天使は現代の教会に集まり、リーダーのメタトロンを待っています。メタトロンが登場して、「人と人との愛情を奨励する」のだと天使に集会の目的を告げます。若い男女を主に励ますことになるが、教会で出会ったこの2人は、互いに相手が好きかどうかわかりません。この2人に姿が見えない天使は、歌と踊りで励ますが、2人にメッセージが伝わらないのです。とうとう、メタトロンは2人に「説教」します。恋人たちは姿が見えないメタトロンの言葉を理解し、彼が最後に考えたことを口にします。「神の天使の仲間になることは、喜びである。」

アルジェント、「靴屋の休日」：サイモンのアリア：ラルフのレター・バラード

　「靴屋の休日」は、1600年頃にロンドンでトマス・デッカーにより書かれた同名の劇を脚色したものです。ローランド・レーシー（リンカーン伯爵の甥）は、ロンドン市長の娘であるローズと恋をしています。しかしながら、伯爵も市長も、二人の結婚を望まず、この恋人達を引き離そうと企てます。レーシーは軍隊に入って戦うよう外国へ派遣されますが、逃亡し、オランダ人に変装してロンドンに返り、市長の靴屋であるサイモン・エアに雇われます。レーシーとローズは再会して、結婚しようと再度計画を立てます。これは、サイモン・エアが市長になった後はずっと簡単となり、そこで、レーシーとローズが結婚することに王様の賛意を得ます。
　市長になって、サイモンはアリアを歌います。市長になれたのは、理性ではなく、稀な幸運だと胸を高鳴らせて歌います。
　その一方で、劇の伏線では、サイモンの靴職人の1人であるラルフ・ダンポートを追います。ラルフは軍に徴兵され、若い妻のジェーンと離れになっています。ラルフは傷を負って1人寂しく、ジェーンに「レター・バラード」を書きます。悲しみが次第に、妻に貞節を守るように訴える文章に変わっていきます。ラルフの懸念は当たっていました。ジェーンはラルフが死んだと思って、ロンドンの別の場所に移り、不謹慎な町の紳士に言い寄られていました。このオペラ全体のテーマと一致させるために、ラルフは結婚の寸前にジェーンを取り返します。もちろん、幸運の助けを借りて。

ドミニク・アルジェント、「水鳥の話」：講師

　「水鳥の話」は、ドミニク・アルジェントがチェーホフの「タバコの害」を自由自在に脚色したものです。オードボンによる「アメリカの鳥」は、ユーモアとペーソスに溢れた1幕の独白ドラマです。19世紀後半、ある中年の紳士が水鳥について講義しています。オペラは講師の聴衆に向けて歌っているかのようであります。オードボンはイラストの投射スライドの前で、様々な鳥の習慣を説明しながら、自分自身の人生も、そうとは気づかずに示しています。若い鴨は巣を離れず、ヒレアシシギでは、オスが巣を守ってメスが飛び回ります。最後に、自分は妻の尻に敷かれて、娘には笑われる不幸な男であると暴露します。
アリア「講師」のスピーチの初めに、緊張しきって、びくびくと妻に服従している様子がはっきりと描かれています。その妻は舞台の脇に、冷然として座っています。

ジャック・ビーソン、「ハイデッガー博士の若さの泉」：生命の処方箋

　　　「ハイデッガー博士の若さの泉」は、ナサニエル・ホーソンの短編を脚色した1幕オペラです。19世紀アメリカの素晴らしい物語で、道徳的な教訓を示してします。年老いたハイデッガー博士は、実験に参加してもらうために、非常に年老いている4人の友人を家に招きます。伝説の「若さの泉」から取ったとするフラスコの水を創造し、招待客は全員その水を飲みます。するとあっという間に若返って、若い情熱も戻ってきます。すぐにこの2人の女性と2人の男性は、互いの気を引こうと争い始め、フラスコが倒れて、水がこぼれます。水がこぼれると、また年を取ったので、ハイデッカーの招待客は仰天して悲しみます。
ハイデッガー博士の「生命の処方箋」は、この実験の教訓です。博士は自分の老いた年と知恵に満足します。しかし、友人は気にせず、「若さの泉」を自分で探そうと誓うのです。

ジャック・ビーソン、「おーい、元気か」：「ギャンブラーの歌」

　　　ジャック・ビーソンの1幕オペラ「おーい、元気か」の舞台はテキサスの小さな町の刑務所です。このオペラでは、急速に花開くロマンスが、数時間後には悲痛な悲劇で結末を迎えます。若者がテキサスのマタドールの獄中で目覚めます。無実のレイプ罪で告訴されて、近くの町ホイーリングで叩きのめされていました。その他の登場人物は、刑務所のコックである少女で、2人は急速に惹かれあいます。互いに寂しいと打ち明け、ギャンブラーは少女をサンフランシスコに連れて行くと言います。「ギャンブラーの歌」では、期待を込めて未来を歌います。
ギャンブラーはホイーリングの男たちに発見されて殺されることを恐れ、少女に銃を取りに行かせます。その間に、男たちが現れてギャンブラーを打ちます。少女が戻ってくると、ギャンブラーは死んでおり、少女はまた孤独に沈み込みます。

レナード・バーンシュタイン、ミサ：「シンプル・ソング」

　　　レナード・バーンシュタインのミサ(1971)は、ローマ・カトリックのミサに基づいています。ある司祭が信仰の危機を経験中で、その司祭の観点から見ています。礼拝の進行は祈祷書通りに行われるが、司祭と信徒の言葉や妨害と並行して演じられ、まるで討論のようであります。
司祭の信仰心は、願いを込め、神を讃えて歌う「シンプル・ソング」で見られるように、最初はシンプルで純粋であります。しかし、人間の不幸の重みや腐敗、権力の虚飾を前に、信仰心は徐々に崩れて行きます。最後に司祭は、まさに信仰心を放棄する寸前で、神を褒め称える他の信仰者と集う喜びに、疑いから生じる孤独はかなわないことに気づきます。

レナード・バーンシュタイン：タヒチでの災難：*この世に摂理あり*

　「タヒチでの災難」は、レナード・バーンシュタインの１幕オペラで、1951年に自分で歌詞を書いて作成されました。一見アメリカン・ドリームを具現しているかのような夫婦の苦悩と孤独を表しています。脚本は、夫婦のある１日の論争と欲求不満を示し、ジャズ・シンガーのトリオが、郊外に家族で住む生活の美徳を褒め称えます。
　サムがダイナと結婚して、10年近くなり、２人の間には９歳の息子がいます。息子は今日の午後、学校の劇で主役を演じることになっています。サムはダイナと息子について議論し、劇を見ずにジムでハンドボールのトーナメントをしようと言って譲らないのです。勝ってハンドボールのトロフィーを獲得した後、ロッカー室で、「この世に摂理あり」というアリアを歌います。うぬぼれて有頂天になり、家族から離れていることを一時的に忘れて、自分は人生の勝利者だと高らかに歌い上げます。

フロイド、「冷たくて厚かましい木」：*ラッカーの説教；君のことが好きなんだと自分でもわかっていた*

　オリーブ・アン・バーンズの小説に基づいている「冷たくて厚かましい木」は、カーライル・フロイトのオペラです。頑固で風変わりな店主で祖父である、ラッカー・ラティンモアを中心に展開します。1900年、ジョージアの「冷たくて厚かましい木」がある町で、最近ラッカーの妻が、長患いの末、亡くなりました。ラッカーは妻の死から３週間後に、ラブ・シンプソンとの結婚を発表して、ラッカーの家族にショックを与えました。ラブは、ラッカーの店で婦人用帽子を販売しており、ラッカーの半分の年齢であった。家族を安心させようと、ラッカーはこう説明します。「結婚は形だけのもの」。ラブが自分の面倒をみて、その代わり、ラブがラッカーの家と家具を相続するのだと。
　ラッカーの家族はラブとの結婚に耐えたが、「冷たくて厚かましい木」の他の住人は、あからさまに嫌がったのです。ラッカーが初めてラブと孫息子のウィルを教会に行かせると、露骨に信徒たちは敵意を示しました。ラブとウィルは直ちに教会を去り、２人が家に帰ると、ラッカーはラブと自分を尊敬している孫息子だけのために、教会の礼拝を自分で実施しようと決意しました。ラッカーの説教では、心の狭い宗教的狂信者について、歯に衣を着せずに述べています。そして、こう結論づけている。神は、男女が自分の人生を大切にして、満喫することをお望みであると。
　形だけの結婚は快適に続き、ラッカーは家の中に配管設備も備え付けて、ラブを驚かせます。ラッカーは配管設備の設置をずっと嫌がっていたからです。ラブの嬉しそうな反応に動かされて、ラッカーは遂にラブのことが好きだと認めます。アリア「君のことが好きなんだと自分でわかっていた」で、ラッカーは最初からラブが好きだった、本当の妻になってほしいと告白します。

　　カーライル・フロイト、ネズミと男：*ジョージのアリア*

　「ネズミと男」は、カーライル・フロイトがジョン・スタインベックの古典的小説1937をオペラ風に脚色したものです。大恐慌の北カルフォルニアで、ジョージ・ミルトンとレニー・スモールという２人の移民労働者が、様々な農場で職を転々としています。レニーは大柄な男だったが、頭の回転がのろく、自分の屈強さに気づかなかったのです。ジョージが献身的にずっとレニーの面倒を見ており、２人には夢があったのです。いつか一緒に農場を経営することです。しかし、レニーの屈強さが悲劇を招いたので、結局、夢は実現しなかったのです。
　２人が新しい宿泊所に到着してすぐ、ジョージは新聞広告で、１ヶ月働けば買えるような安い農場を見つけました。農場の経験豊かな現場監督であるスリムは、ジョージが広告をしげしげと眺めているのを見て、その夢を思いとどまらせようとしました。スリムは多くの農場労働者が夢を追って、苦い失望を味わっているのを知っています。ジョージは、むきになってアリアでこう応えます。レニーは放浪と孤独以上のものを人生で見つけるだろうと強硬に言い張るのです。

カーライル・フロイト、「ジョナサン・ウェイドの情熱」：*眠れ、良心よ、眠れ*

　　　舞台は、南北戦争の終わり、南カロライナのコロンビアの黒っぽい廃墟であります。カーライル・フロイトの「ジョナサン・ウエィド」は悲劇です。南部の難しい再建を脅かしたのと同じ力が、ある男の人生を引き裂いたのです。ジョナサン・ウェイドは北軍の大佐で、コロンビアを監督する将校として、コロンビアに到着します。ジョナサンは暴力に訴え妥協を知らない反乱軍に手を焼いています。その一方で、北軍の政治家は、自分の政治力を高めようと、状況を利用します。そうこうするうちに、ジョナサンは、地元の判事の娘であるセリア・タウンセンドと恋をします。
　　　ところが、ワシントンはタウンセンド判事を解任するように、ジョナサンに指示し、ジョナサンの心は迷います。命令に従うと、セリアと判事を裏切ることになります。判事は、ジョナサンに寛容で優しかったのです。「眠れ、良心よ、眠れ」は、果たすべき義務で苦しまないように、ジョナサンが良心に嘆願している歌です。

フロイド、スザンナ：*「主よ、聞きたまえ。」*

　　　カーライル・フロイトの「スザンナ」は、オペラ以上のものです。アメリカ南部が舞台だが、米国全体や海外も描いています。20世紀半ば、テネシー山脈にある人里離れたニューホープ峡谷の共同体で、スザンナ・ポークは兄のサムと住んでいます。スザンナは若く、輝くように美しいです。そのため、最近教会に現れた激烈なオリン・ブリッチなど周りの人々は、スザンナの純潔を疑っています。入り江で水浴しているところを密かに見られた後、教会の長老は、姦通したとスザンナを徹底的に非難して、共同体から追放しました。ブリッチはスザンナに圧力をかけて良心の呵責を味わさせようと、スザンナの家に来たものの、そうせずにスザンナに対する自分の欲望を満たしてしまったのです。スザンナはひどく取り乱して疲れていて、抵抗できなかったのです。
　　　翌朝ブリッチは、1人教会で「良心の呵責の祈り」を歌います。スザンナの純潔と自分の罪の重さを悟ったが、既に遅かったのです。信徒が来たときに、ブリッチは自分がスザンナと親しくなったことを認めずに、スザンナを許すように懇願したが、信徒はスザンナの純潔を信じません。許しは与えられませんでした。というのは、狩の旅行から帰ってスザンナの話を聞いたサムが、怒り来るってブリッチを殺したからです。

カーライル・フロイト、「ウィリー・スターク」：*毛布1枚；我らは皆、地面から生まれる*

　　　「ウィリー・スターク」は、カーライル・フロイトが、ロバート・ペン・ウォレンの小説「オール・ザ・キングス・メン」を脚色したものです。この小説は、南部の知事の興亡を描いた物語です。スタークは、その人民的な思想で田舎の貧しい人々に愛され、情けを知らぬ機動作戦で国家の政治組織に憎まれています。スタークの政治的地位は強大であるが、自分に近い人々の生活に対して、スタークの個性が示す圧倒的な存在感も、同じくらい強烈です。
　　　国会議事堂で白熱した戦いが行われています。スタークの政治的な敵が、スタークに対して弾劾という戦いを開始しています。スタークが社会改革のために、司法制度を操作したというのです。非常に尊敬されているバードン判事が、弾劾の判例を支持しようとしていると聞いたスタークは、止めさせようとバードン判事の自宅を訪れます。判事の答えは短いが、痛烈です。スタークが「法律を軽視している」ので、弾劾を支持するのだと。これに対して、スタークはアリア「毛布1枚」で答えます。庶民の寓話の形で、人民的な視点から法律をどのように見るのかを表しています。
　　　その日、故郷メイソン市の裁判所の階段に、群集が集まっていました。スタークは突然、群集の中でハーモニカを引く若い少年の光景に、心を動かされます。スタークは若い頃を思い出し、少年からハーモニカを買って、「我らは皆、地面から生まれた」を歌います。スタークは、いつもの政治家としてのしたたかさをなくし、今までの人生を思い出します。過去に捨ててきたビジョンを懐かしく思いながら。

ムーア、「悪魔とダニエル・ウェブスター」：*雄羊を手に入れたよ、ゴリアテ*

　「*悪魔とダニエル・ウェブスター*」は、1840年代のニューハンプシャーを舞台にし、悪魔に対し聡明なアメリカ人弁護士で政治家である男が戦います。ウェブスターは、継続的な貧困から不思議にも抜け出し州議会の議員に昇って来たジェービズ・ストーンの結婚式で貴賓となります。その祝典は、邪悪なスクラッチ（やがて後に悪魔であることを明かします）によって中断されます。ジェービズは、10年前に自分の魂を前もって売ったと認めますが、ウェブスターは、その件に反論することを申し出ます。スクラッチが自分で選んだ陪審団（地獄から連れ戻された悪名高い裏切り者で構成されています）は、ウェブスターの法律的主張を妨害しますが、ウェブスターは、命と自由への彼の上告によって彼らさえも勝ち取ります。ジェービズ・ストーンは結婚し、大喜びの地元民はニューハンプシャーから悪魔を追い出します。
　アリア「雄羊を手に入れたよ、ゴリアテ」で、ウェブスターは農夫としての強さと、自由を求める決意を歌い上げます。

ネッド・ローレム、「強盗」：*木霊は盗めない*

　ネッド・ローレムの「*強盗*」は、チョーサーによるカンタベリー物語の「パードナーの物語」を脚色した1幕オペラです。3人の追いはぎが、旅人を民宿の部屋に招き入れて殺し、金を手に入れます。強盗の1人は若くて未熟で、殺人に震えています。他の2人は貪欲さに動かされ、この新米がうっかり犯罪を漏らすのではないかと心配して、その夜遅く、新米を殺そうとしています。
　新米はまだ殺人について、じっくり考えています。新米が歌うアリア「木霊は盗めない」で、心配が徐々に邪悪な発想に変わっていきます。他の2人を殺せば、金は全て自分の物になるのです。
　新米はワインのボトルに毒を入れて、仲間に渡します。2人は新米を殺して、ワインを飲みます。こうして4人の死体と散らばった金の上に、幕が下ります。

ストラヴィンスキー、「道楽者の進歩」：*ニック・シャドーのアリア*

　ストラヴィンスキーは、ハリウッド在住当時の1951年に、素晴らしい新古典オペラ「道楽者の進歩」を執筆した。W.H. オーデンの歌詞では、トム・レイクウェルの物語を語ります。トムは怠け者の若い男性で、実力ではなく、幸運によって人生を生きていこうと決意しています。邪悪なニック・シャドーが現れ、見知らぬ叔父が遺産を残したと伝えます。トムはニックと一緒にロンドンに行き、相続問題を片付け、アン・ツルーラブを呼び寄せようとします。しかし、性格的に弱いトムは、全ての美徳を捨てさせられて自滅し、簡単にシャドーの餌食になってしまいます。
　トムはロンドンに着いてすぐ、不満を感じて不幸せになります。シャドーはトムに異常な提案をします。トムが、欧州全域で有名なひげ女、ベイバ・ザ・タークと結婚すべきだと言うと、トムの反応は懐疑的であったが、シャドーはずる賢いアリアで、トムに計画を納得させます。男は不自由だと不幸なのだ。自由になるには、理性と欲望を捨てねばならぬと。

Dewain's Song of Liberation and Surprise

from I WAS LOOKING AT THE CEILING AND THEN I SAW THE SKY

Act II

Text by
JUNE JORDAN

Music by
JOHN ADAMS
(1995)

I saw the moon in the morn-ing _____ I felt the wa-ter on dry land _

I saw the moon in the morn-ing I found the riv-er _____ in the sand

And the walls shook and they fell __ And I heard the shat-ter-ing

M-051-93366-2

2

3

4

ground was weird and in - com - plete

And so I stood

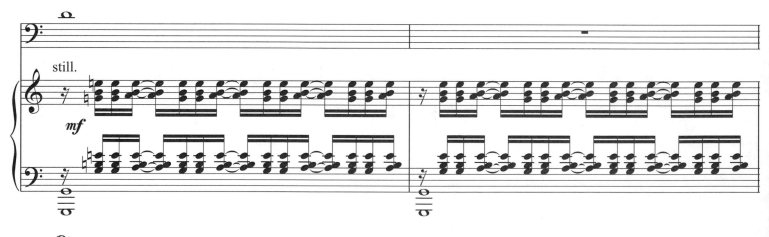

still,_____ And so I stood still,_____ stood

gradual diminuendo

still.

A very slight relaxation of tempo ♩ =72

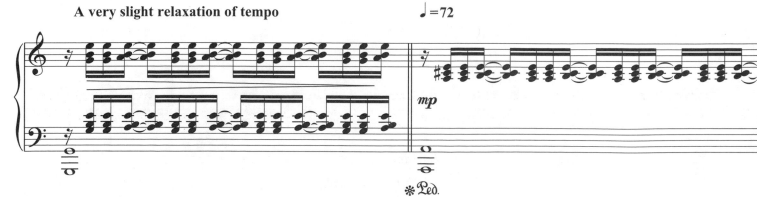

free!"

Rall. _ _ _ _ _ _

A tempo

"I am the way,

I am the

way,_____

I am the way

I will be

gradual crescendo

free.＿＿＿＿＿＿＿＿＿＿ I am the

way, I am the way,＿＿＿＿＿＿＿＿＿ I am the

way, I will be free.＿＿＿＿＿＿＿＿＿＿

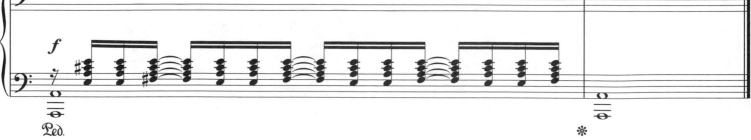

Shake the Heavens
from EL NIÑO
Part I

Text from
Haggai 2:6

Music by
JOHN ADAMS
(2000)

shake   the heav -   -   - ens,

For_____ thus sa - ith the Lord:_____

Ah_____ I will,__ will,___ will___ shake,__

And I will shake, shake,_____ I__ will__ shake,__ shake,_____ I will shake__ the__

heav - ens,__ I will__ shake the heav - ens, and the earth,_____

and the sea,_____ and the dry land:__ It is a

lit - tle while__ and I will shake the heav - ens, I will

shake the dry land: And I will shake the earth, I will

shake, shake, I will shake the dry land: And the

sea, the sea, the sea, the sea, I will, I will,

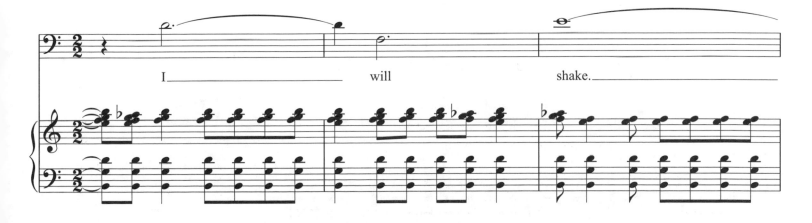

I will shake.

14

And the de - sire of all___ the na -

- tions, and the de - sire of all___ the na - tions shall___ come:

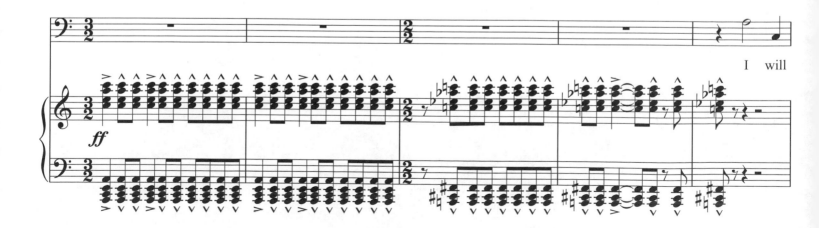

I will

shake_____

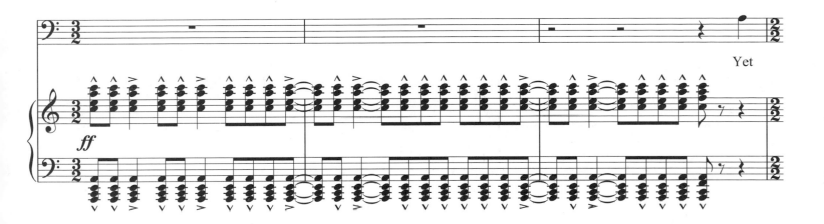

Yet

once,   it is a lit-tle while,   and I will shake   the heav - - ens.__

Dawn Air
from EL NIÑO
Part II

Text by
VICENTE HUIDOBRO

Music by
JOHN ADAMS
(2000)

tell,   tell,   tell   the   shep - herds,

Tell   the   shep - herds   the   wind   is   sad - dling   its

horse,___   The   wind   is   sad - dling   its

horse_____   And   wav - ing_____   as   it

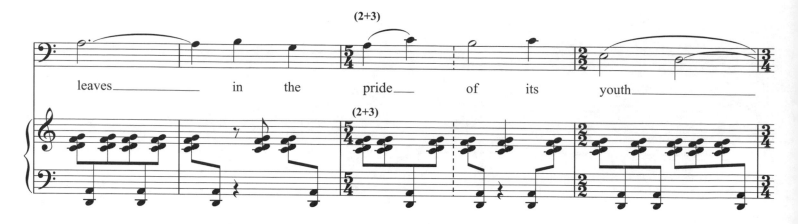

leaves_____ in the pride___ of its youth_____

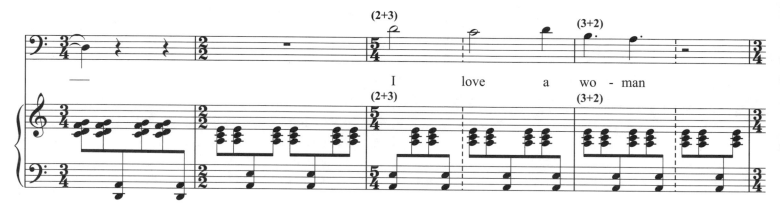

___ I love a wo - man

proud and dream - like Si - lent

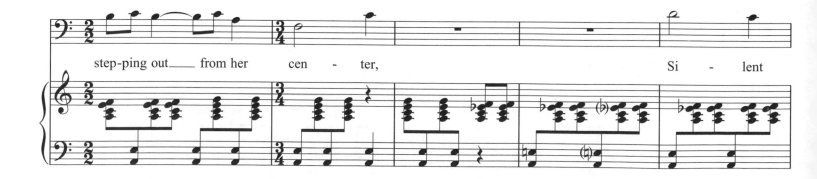

step-ping out___ from her cen - ter, Si - lent

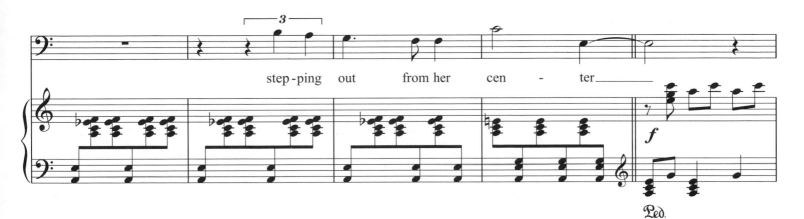

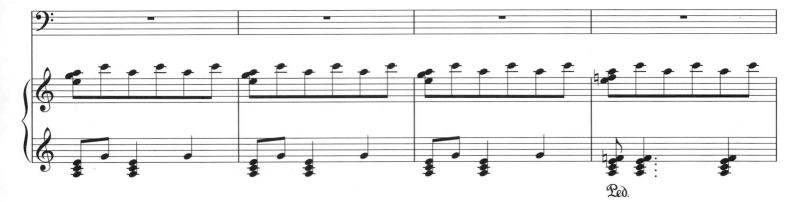

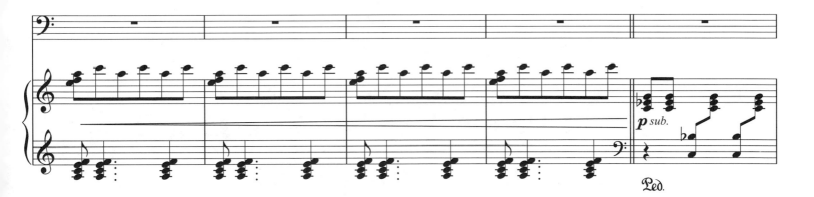

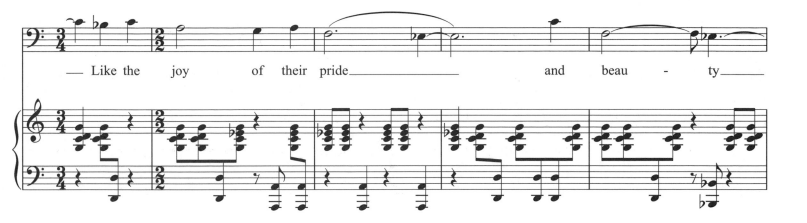

— Like the joy of their pride＿＿＿＿ and beau - ty＿＿＿

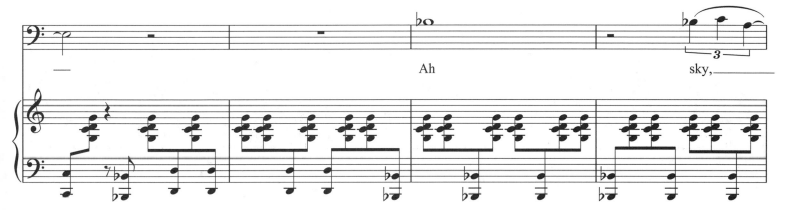

Ah sky,＿＿＿

Ah,＿＿＿＿＿

sky＿ blue＿ for the queen＿ in the wind＿＿＿＿

(con Ped.)

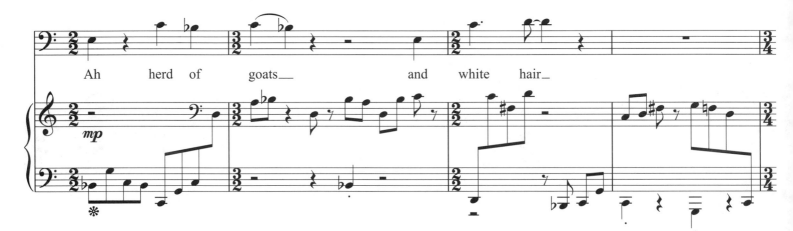

Ah herd of goats_____ and white hair__

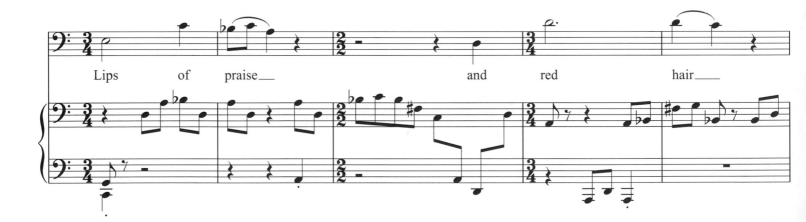

Lips of praise_____ and red hair____

An - i - mals lost in her eyes_____

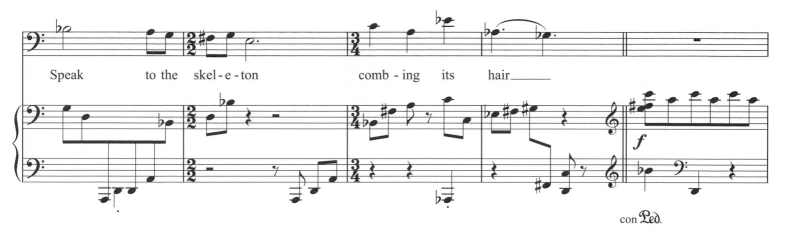

Speak to the skel-e-ton comb-ing its hair_____

con Ped.

con Ped.

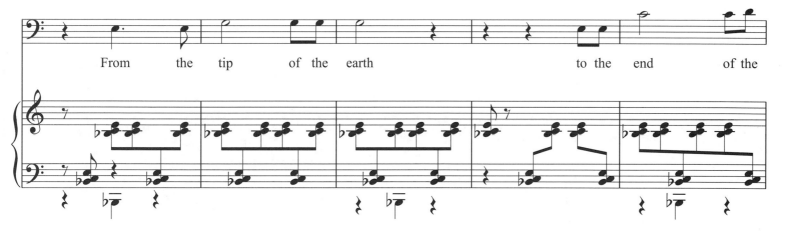

From the tip of the earth to the end of the

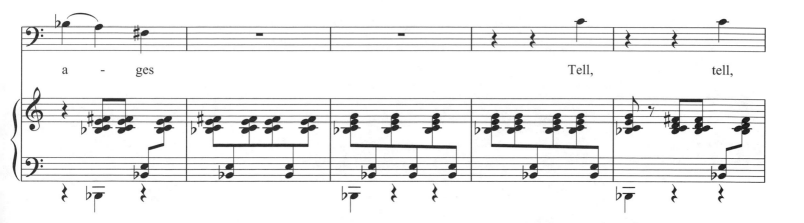

a - ges Tell, tell,

24

sound of high - ways   Speak   to the land

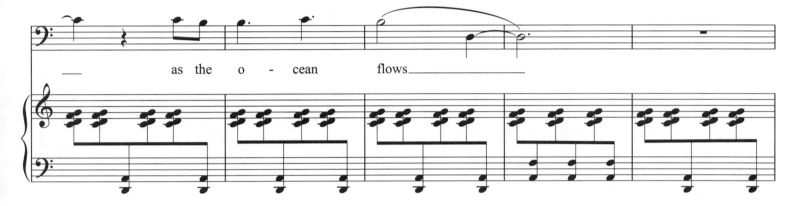

as the o - cean   flows

Ah,   ah,   ah,   ah,   the

wind,   the   wind,

26

the wind stops for the queen,____

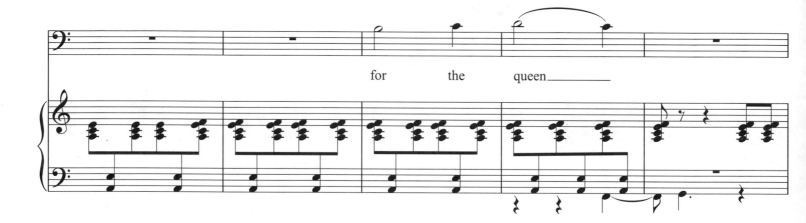

for the queen_____

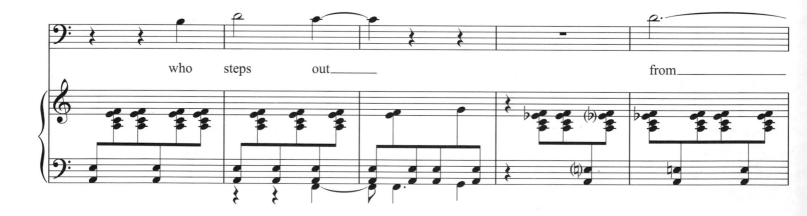

who steps out_____ from_____

____ her sky_____

News has a kind of mystery

from NIXON IN CHINA
Act I, Scene 1

Text by
ALICE GOODMAN

Music by
JOHN ADAMS
(1987)

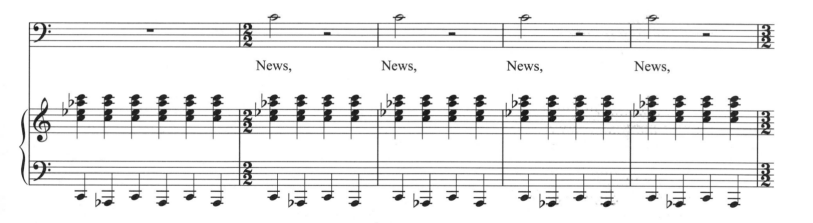

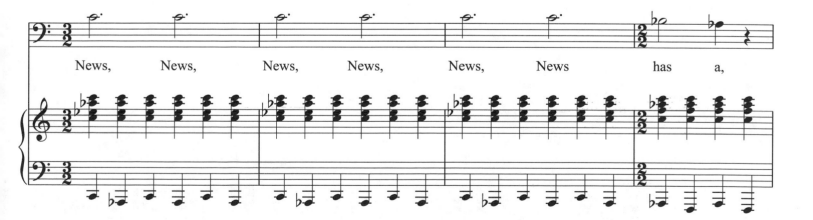

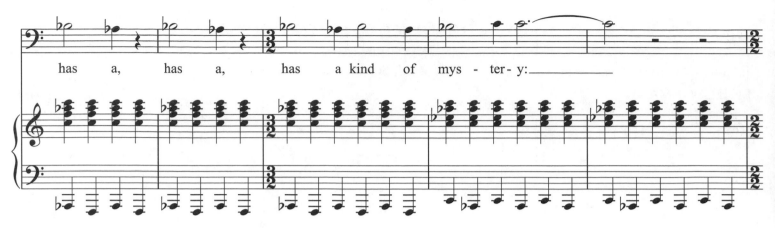

has a, has a, has a kind of mys - ter - y:_____

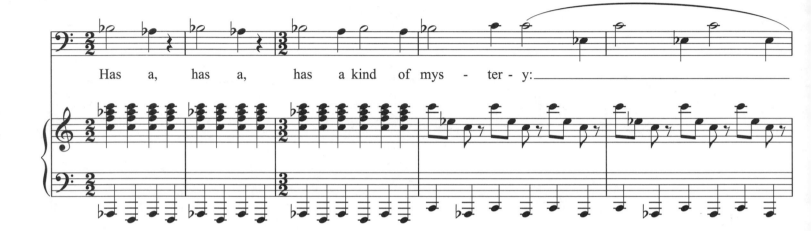

Has a, has a, has a kind of mys - ter - y:_____

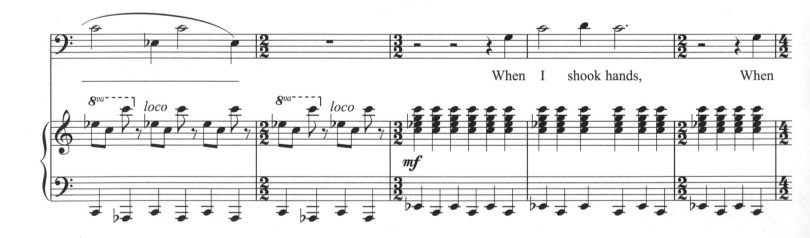

When I shook hands, When

I shook hands____ with Chou En-lai, When I shook hands with Chou En-lai on

this bare field out - side Pe-king_ just now, the whole world was lis-ten-ing.

The whole world was lis - ten-ing. Lis - ten-ing.

Lis - ten - ing. And

though we spoke qui - et - ly, And though we spoke

gesss - ture– Caught ev - ery gesss - ture and ev - ery

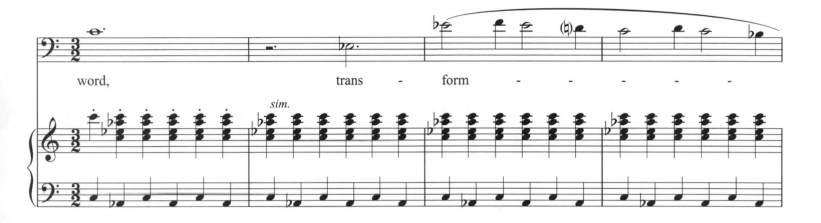

word, trans - form - - - - -

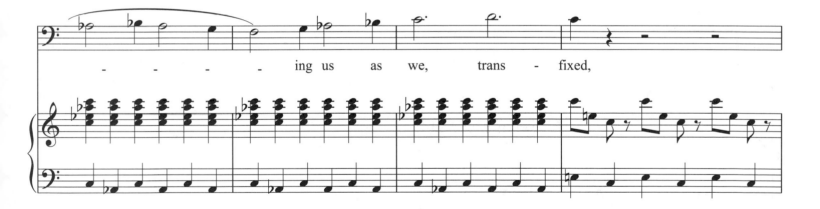

- - - - ing us as we, trans - fixed,

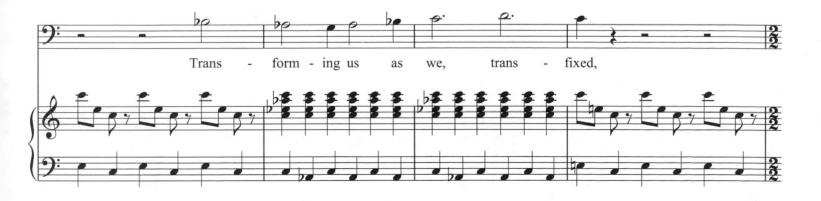

Trans - form - ing us as we, trans - fixed,

32

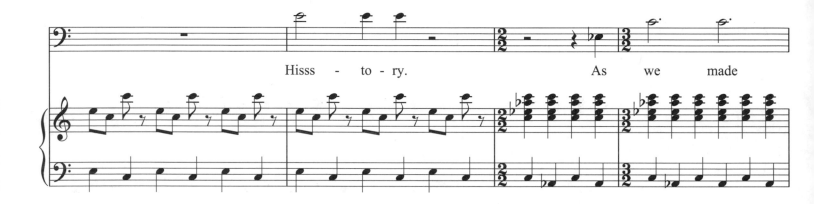

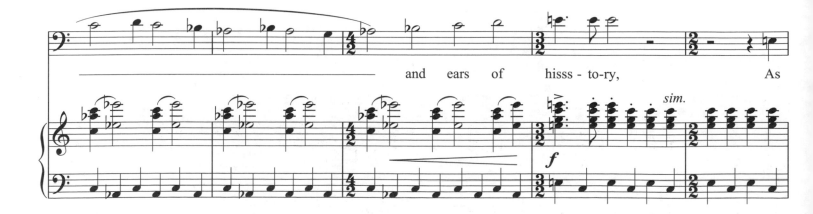

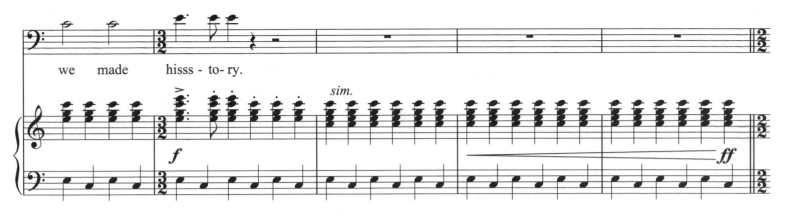

we made hisss-to-ry.

On our flight___ o - ver from Shang -

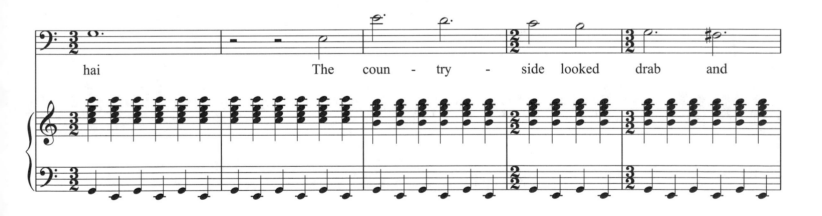

hai   The coun - try - side looked drab and

grey.   "Brue-ghel,"   Pat   said.

34

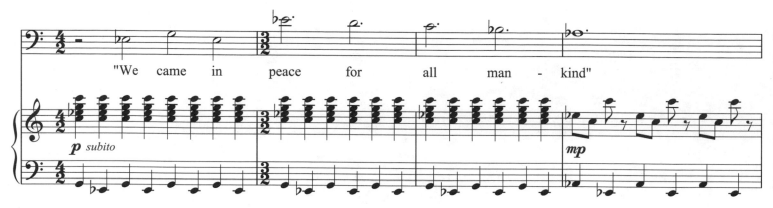

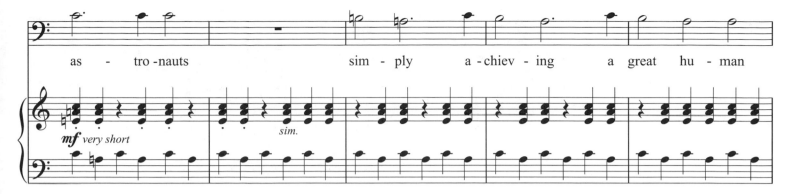

as - tro -nauts   sim - ply   a -chiev - ing   a   great   hu - man

dream.   We   live

in   an   un -set - tled   time.

We   live   in   an   un -set - tled   time.

36

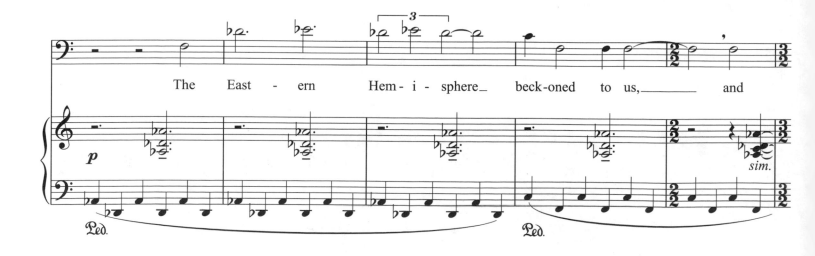

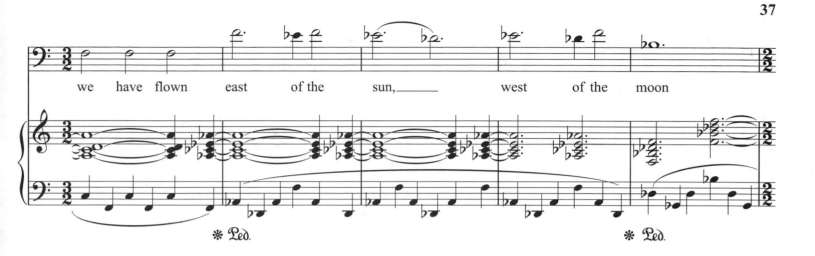

we have flown east of the sun,_____ west of the moon

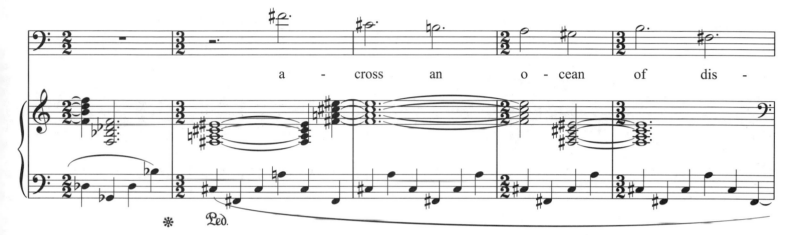

a - cross an o - cean of dis -

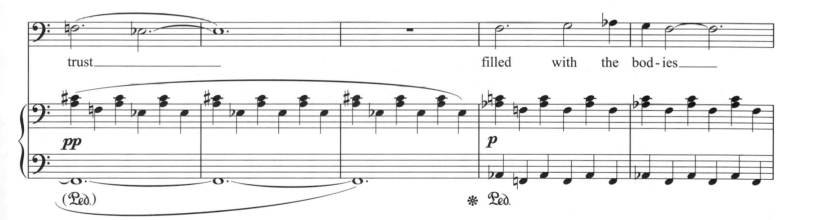

trust_____ filled with the bod - ies_____

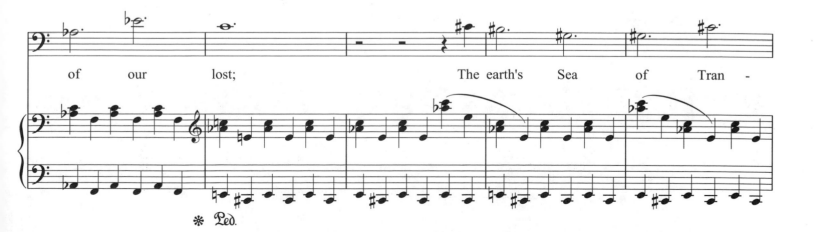

of our lost; The earth's Sea of Tran -

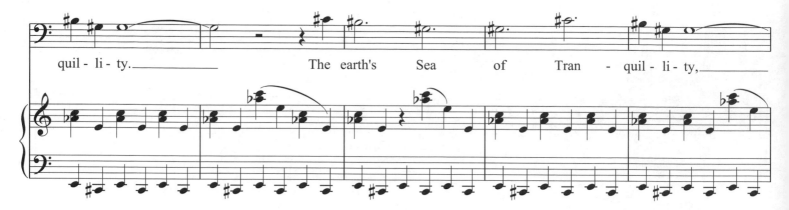

quil - li - ty._____ The earth's Sea of Tran - quil - li - ty,_____

_____ Tran - quil - li - ty,_____ The

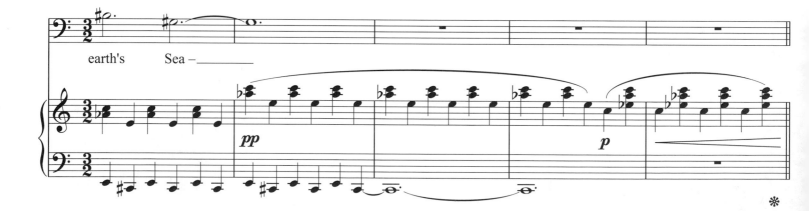

earth's Sea –_____

News! News! News! News! News!

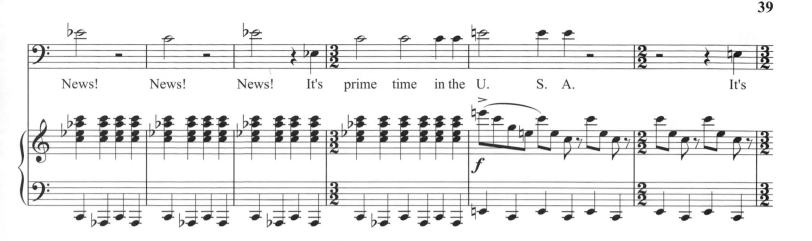

News! News! News! It's prime time in the U. S. A. It's

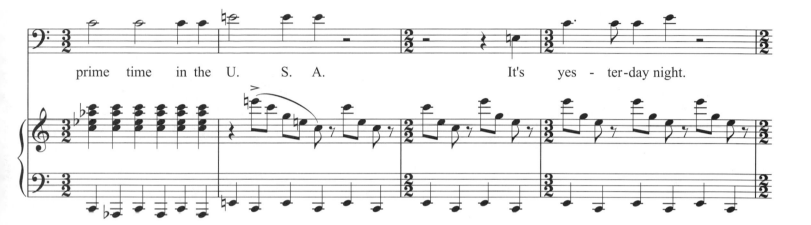

prime time in the U. S. A. It's yes - ter-day night.

It's yes - ter-day night. Yes - ter-day night. They

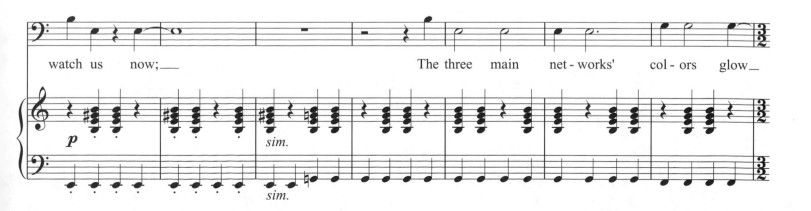

watch us now;___ The three main net - works' col - ors glow___

Relax tempo slightly, but not suddenly (♩=144)

As I look down the road I know A -

mer - i - ca is good at heart. An

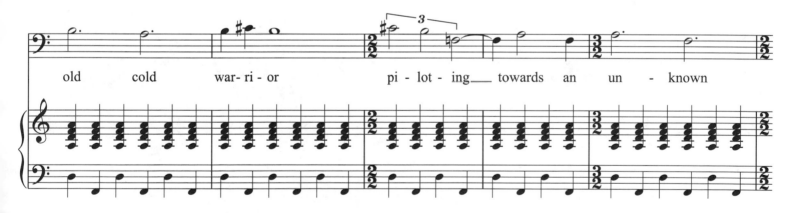

old cold war- ri - or pi - lot - ing towards an un - known

shore through shoals.

Gradual relaxation of tempo

There's mur-mur-ing,   There's mur-mur-ing,   mur-mur-ing.   Now there's in-

-gra-ti-tude!   My hand is____ as stead-y as a rock.

A sound like mourn-ing doves____

♩ = 138 Steady tempo

reach-es my ears,____   No-bod-y is____ a friend of____ ours.____

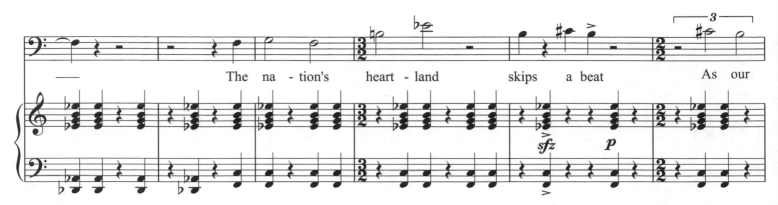

The na-tion's heart-land skips a beat   As our

hands   shield the spin-ning globe___   from the flame-throw-ers___

___   of the   mob.   We   must   press on.

Begin gradual relaxation of tempo

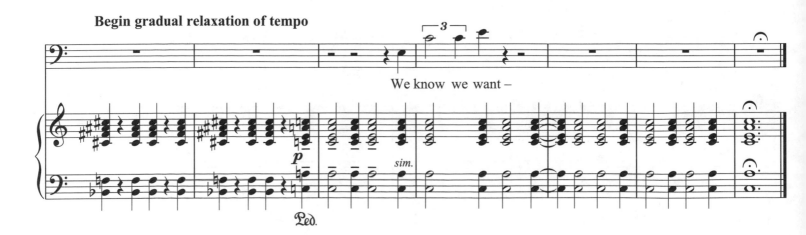

We know we want –

Chou En-lai's Epilogue

from NIXON IN CHINA
Act II, Scene 2

Text by
ALICE GOODMAN

Music by
JOHN ADAMS
(1987)

I am old____ and can-not sleep for - ev - er,____ like the young,

nor hope that death will be a nov-el-ty____ but

end - less____ wake-ful-ness when I put down my

46

work and go_____ to bed.

Ped.

How much of what we did was good?

(p)

p

Ped.

Ped.

Ev-ry-thing_____ seems_____ to move be-yond our

re - me - dy._____   Come,

heal this wound.   At

A little slower and freely played

this hour_____ noth - ing_____ can be done.

48

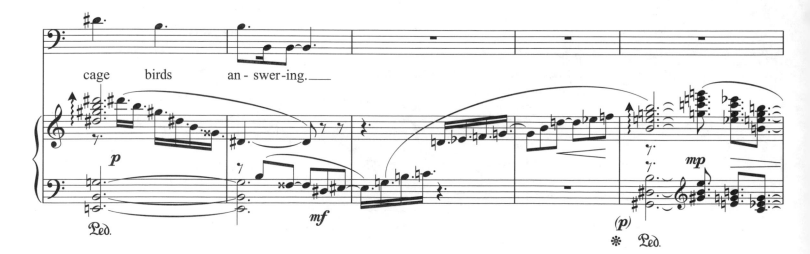

To work!

Out -side this room   the chill of

grace   lies heav - y   on   the morn - ing grass.

poco rall.

Boor's Aria

from THE BOOR
Scene 6

Text by
JOHN OLON-SCRYMGEOUR

Music by
DOMINICK ARGENTO
(1957)

Thank you ver- y much! Thank you ver- y much!

What is a man_____ sup - posed_____ to do?_____ They'll see you hanged be-fore they're

through._____ You ask for help___ and you're treat-ed to__ "A state of

mind!" They al-ways tell me I nev-er smile,

That my man-ner's gruff, my tem-per vile, Their hands in my pock-et all the while

And I'm to blame! And I'm to blame! Now, I'm a friend-ly sort of man

Good - na - tured and po-lite. I come up to a friend, hold out my hand

In a min-ute he is out of sight!

Trou-ble is I'm too kind,_____ kind:_____ All you get for a

good turn is a state of mind, a state of mind, a state of mind!_____

friend_____ is ill,_____ an-oth-er's_____ a - way_____ I tip my hat__ and come

One

back next day._____ The treat - ment's the same,___ and what___ do they

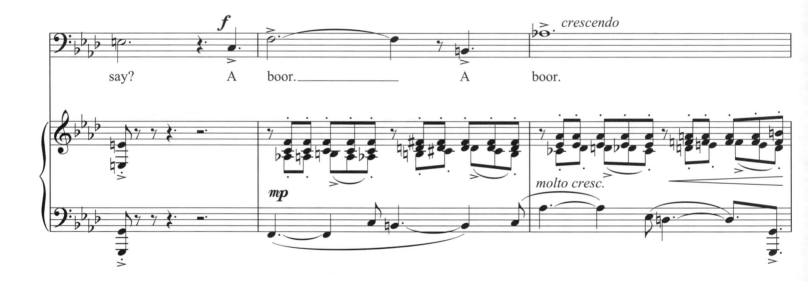

say? A boor._____ A boor.

Cadenza

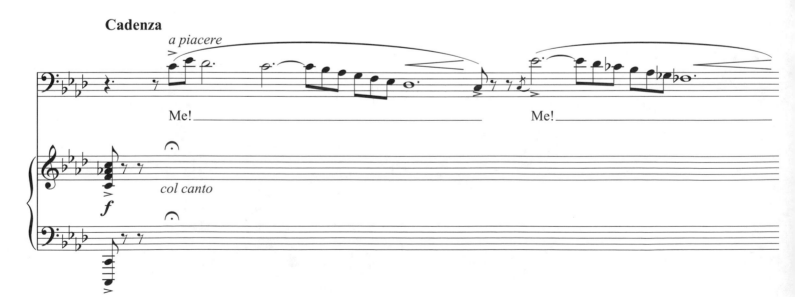

Me!_____ Me!_____

Me! Me,— Me,— Me,— Me! A—

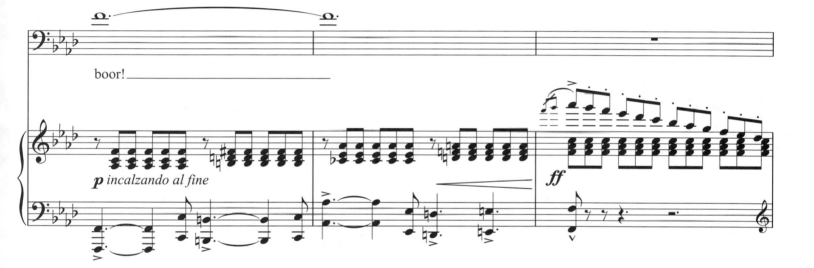

boor!

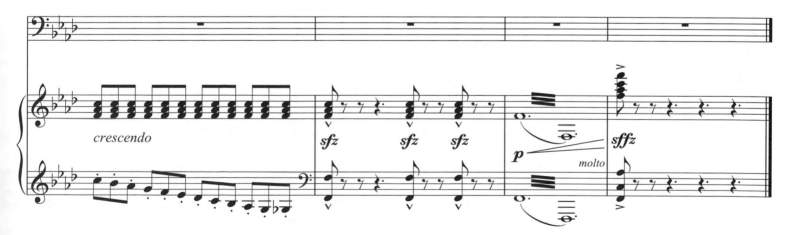

Casanova's Final Air

from CASANOVA'S HOMECOMING
Act III

Text and Music by
DOMINICK ARGENTO
(1984)

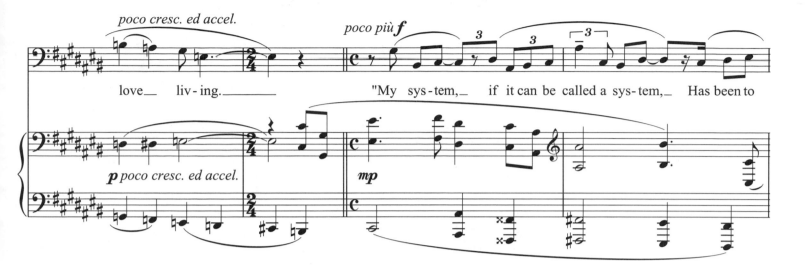

love__ liv - ing._____ "My sys-tem,__ if it can be called a sys-tem,__ Has been to

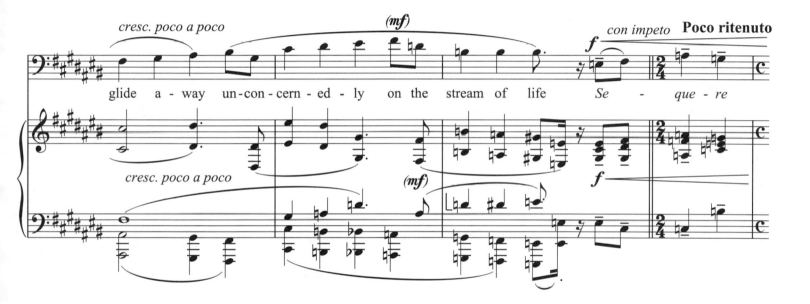

glide a - way un-con-cern-ed - ly on the stream of life Se - que - re

De - um–   Trust-ing__ to the wind____ wher-ev - ver_____ it

58

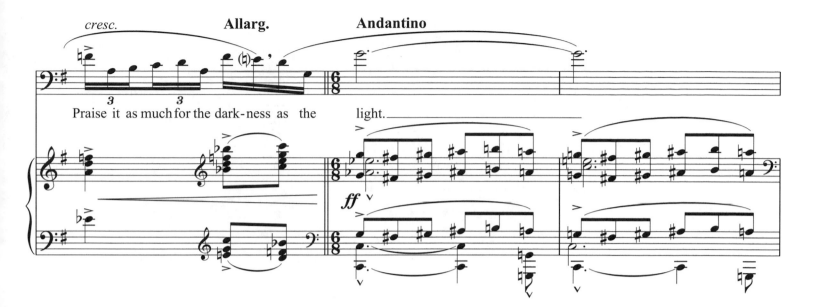

Praise it as much for the dark-ness as the light.

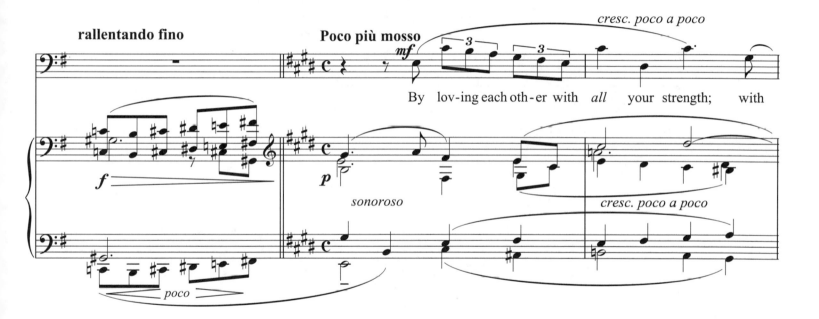

By lov-ing each oth-er with *all* your strength; with

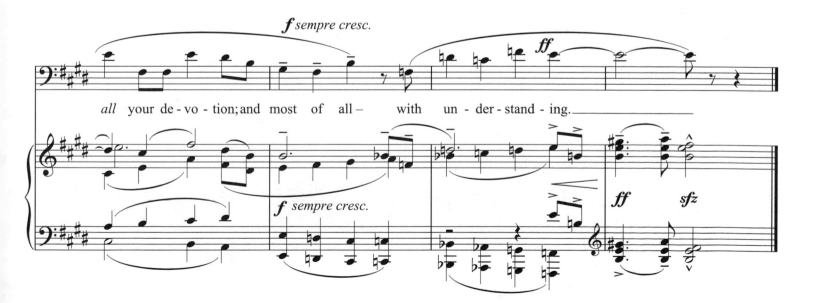

all your de-vo-tion; and most of all— with un-der-stand-ing.

Sly's Aria

from CHRISTOPHER SLY
Scene 2

Text by
JOHN MANLOVE

Music by
DOMINICK ARGENTO
(1962)

be not clawed yer - self!

"Wilt please yer hon - or?..." Thank ye, thank ye, thank ye! "A sil - ver gob - let?..."

Aye, that a' will! "Wilt please yer lord - ship?..." Thank ye, thank ye, thank ye! "A sack o' mon - ey?..."

want is ful - filled!" If a' don't clean ye out like a cly - ster pipe, Cut off m' ears for a

cheap-side thief! Ye've seen the last of old Chris-to-pher Sly, But praised be God, old Sly will live off

ye un - til his last a - men! And so I thank ye for yer kind-ness; But a' real-ly must a - way.

Metatron's Sermon

from THE MASQUE OF ANGELS

Text by
JOHN OLON-SCRYMGEOUR

Music by
DOMINICK ARGENTO
(1963)

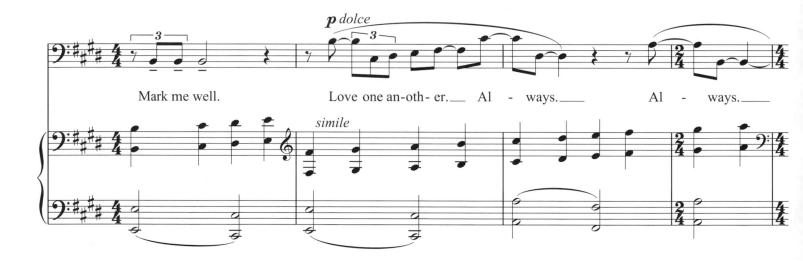

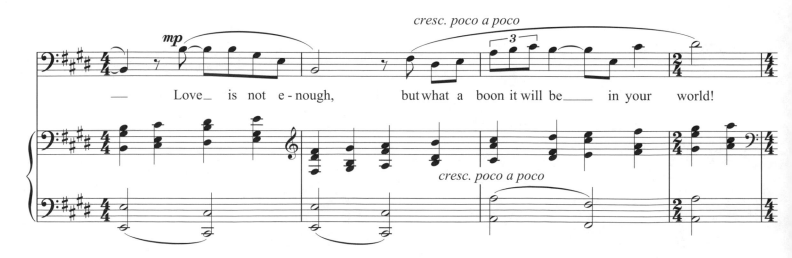

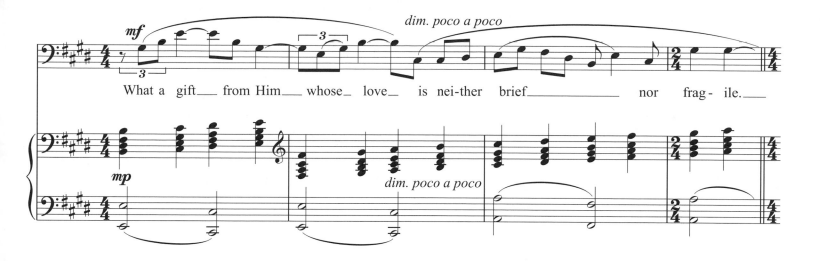

What a gift___ from Him___ whose___ love___ is nei-ther brief_____ nor frag - ile.___

Go now in - to the world be-yond these walls. It will

not be eas - y with you._____ But with your mu-tu - al love I will send U - ri-el___

to light your day. And Lei-lah,__ go and make their nights soft and

dark. Ga-bri-el, fol-low af-ter them and rip-en the fruit of their

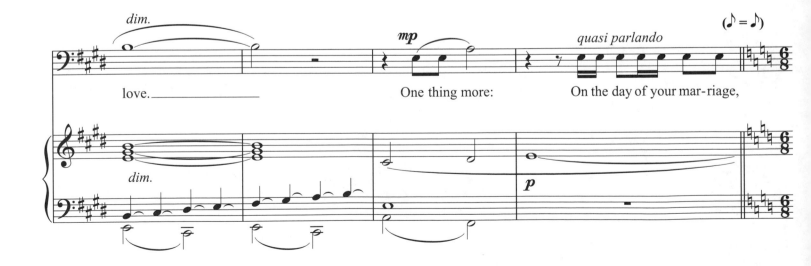

love._____ One thing more: On the day of your mar-riage,

a stran-ger will nod to you and smile—__ an old__ maid in a fad-ed

hat. She will stop you in the midst__

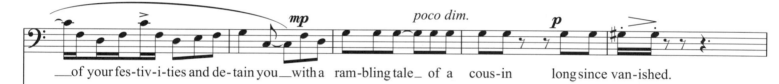

__of your fes-tiv-i-ties and de-tain you__with a ram-bling tale__ of a cous-in long since van-ished.

Al-low your-selves neith-er a smile of de - ri-sion or pit-y.

col pedale sempre

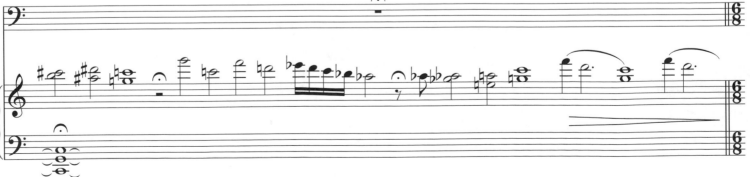

Lat-er   in the midst of your trials,___ some young boy may come to you com-plain-ing___ of his

faith-less love.   In your anx-i-e-ty___ don't turn a - way._____

Ir - ri - ta-tion and Dis -trac-tion: These are oth-er names___ for Thrones and Dom-i - na - tions___

Come sopra

___ and they will   help you   like branch-es on a hill_____ or___ foun-tains and

rall.

bird_ song_ in a des-ert place to face this Trial of Time._____

poco cresc. e rall.

Larghetto (Tempo I)

mp

_ And we– poor fowls of the air, we_will nev-er leave you, though some-times you leave

simile

p

poco cresc.

us. And in the midst of your se-ver-est woe, re - mem-ber this–_____ But I shall not say it,_

poco cresc.

mp

poco cresc.

mf

for I see it al-read-y on your lips._____

poco cresc.

mf

dim. *p* *dim.*

Ralph's Letter-Ballad

from THE SHOEMAKERS' HOLIDAY
Scene 12

Text by
JOHN OLON-SCRYMGEOUR
after the play by Thomas Decker

Music by
DOMINICK ARGENTO
(1967)

Più mosso

mf

our couched and bed - ded foes be-lieved We came with an- gry lours;

pesante

sim.

f

mp sub.

Their wis-doms were the more de - ceived:___ Such ha-tred is not ours;___ What

cresc.

f

mp sub.

cresc. e stringendo poco a poco

molto rall.

f

sort of ha-tred can they find In men who left their hearts be - hind?___

molto rall.

cresc. e stringendo poco a poco

f

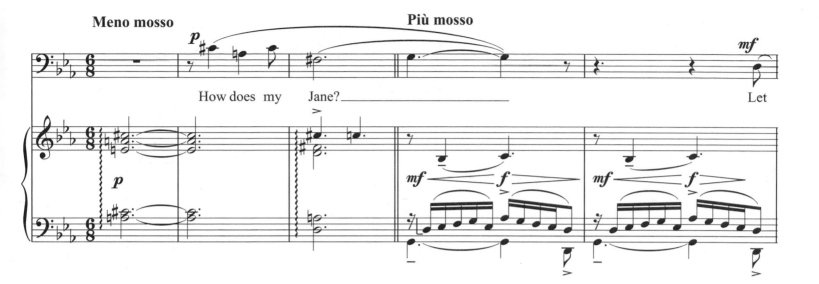

Meno mosso ... **Più mosso**

How does my Jane?_____ Let

wind and weath-er do their worse Be you to us but kind:_____

Let sol-diers va - pour, coun-tries curse,_____ No sor-rows shall we

Simon's Aria

from THE SHOEMAKERS' HOLIDAY
Scene 21

Text by
JOHN OLON-SCRYMGEOUR
after the play by Thomas Decker

Music by
DOMINICK ARGENTO
(1967)

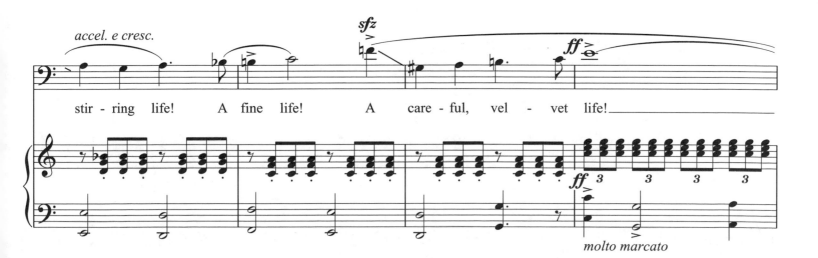

Bright-est can - dles burn a - pace.

a piacere

–But it's a mad life! It's a stir-ring life! It's a fine and

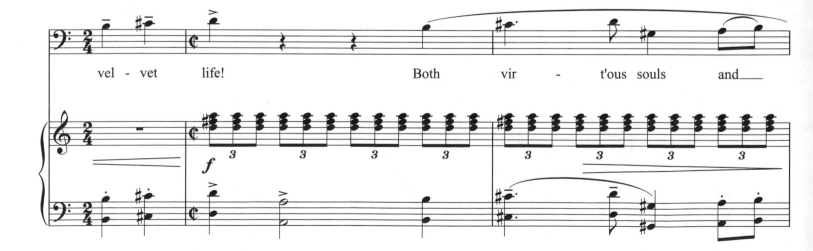

vel - vet life! Both vir - t'ous souls and

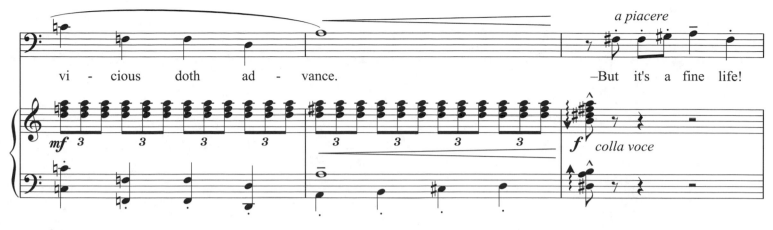

vi-cious doth ad-vance.   –But it's a fine life!

It's a vel-vet life!   It's a mad and stir-ring life!   All men are mad, all

mad, all mad knaves all!   All beg-gars, rogues and

thieves, –yet this mad knave looks soft on all.   Why then does not he grieve?_____

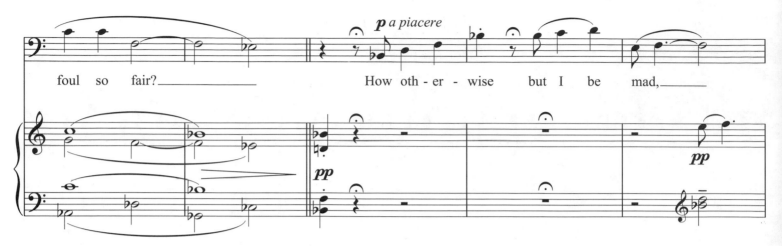

foul so fair?_____ How oth-er-wise but I be mad,_____

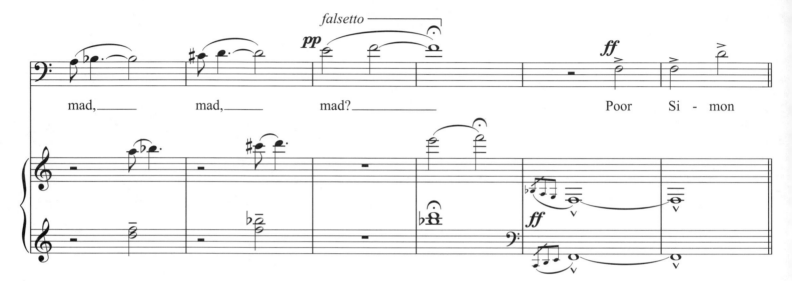

mad,_____ mad,_____ mad?_____ Poor Si - mon

Più mosso che tempo I

Eyre!_____

The Lecturer
from A WATERBIRD TALK

Text and Music by
DOMINICK ARGENTO
(1974-76)

84

Stesso tempo ma espansivo

quasi parlato e senza rigidità

mf legato e cantabile

hold an-y learn-ed de-grees._____ I have, how-ev-er, o-ver the past thir-ty years, de-vel-oped a cer-tain ca-

pac-i-ty for ob-ser-va-tion. More and more, it has be-come my ha-bit sim-ply to...

ob-serve; to ob-serve the world a-bout us and to stud-y all man-ner of things; to try to

un - der - stand___ and to share that un - der - stand - ing with oth - ers. Some years a - go, I com-

posed a ver - y long es - say en - ti - tled: "Scor - pi - ons, Spi - ders and Cen - ti - pedes." My daugh - ters all seemed to en - joy it –

es - pe - cial - ly those sec - tions on spi - der's webs and how they serve as both nest and trap –

ter-ri-ble dread of wa-ter a com-plete-ly ir-ra-tion-al fear of drown-ing. But my wife in-sist-ed:

'Don't you dare em-bar-rass me a - gain— none of your aw-ful bugs: I warn you!'—

So Wa - ter Birds it shall be.

Prescription For Living
from DR. HEIDEGGER'S FOUNTAIN OF YOUTH

Text by
SHELDON HARNICK
after the short story by
NATHANIEL HAWTHORNE

Music by
JACK BEESON
(1978, rev. 1990)

newed my own dis-or-dered youth,___ the hec-tic blood, the blind,___ mer-cu-rial mind._____ I thank the

poco f

Lord I have left that fierce de - lir - i - um___ be - hind.

mp

Mosso, with growing resolution

A little more deliberately (subito a tempo)

mp clearly

Were I to find that just be-yond my

poco f

poco f

mp

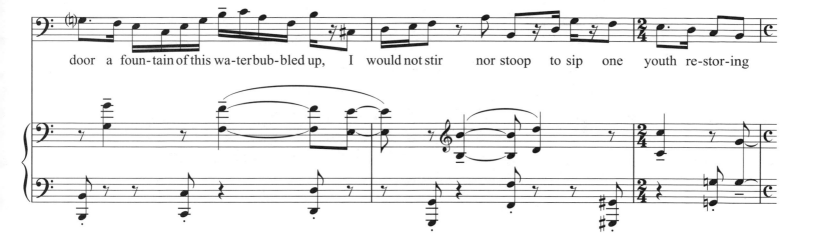

door a foun-tain of this wa-ter bub-bled up, I would not stir nor stoop to sip one youth re-stor-ing

Mosso, affirmatively

cup.

Rallentando   **A tempo ($\quad$ = ca. 46-48)**

fully, resonately

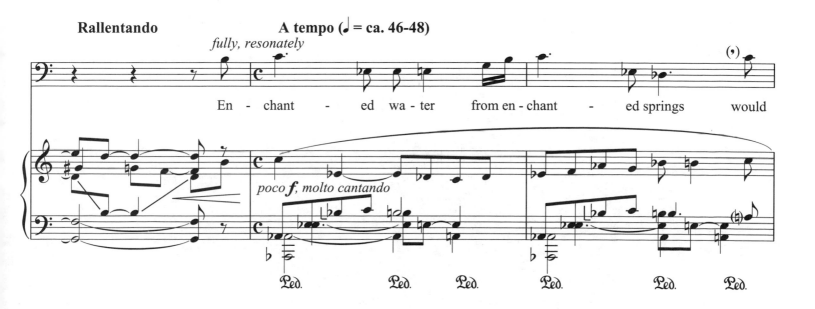

En - chant - ed wa - ter from en - chant - ed springs would

poco f, molto cantando

92

Ritenuto

seem____ to be de-sir - a-ble at first. But, in the end, an hon-est glass of port will more than

Accel. poco a poco

am - ply sat - is - fy my thirst.

Broadly swinging
(♪ = ca. 120) (♩. = ca. 40)

My__ friends,__ my a - ged lads__ and las-sies, if your years__ so lit-tle have taught you, so

lit - tle have brought you,___ if the vast and var - ied rich-ness of life can no long-er fill your

diminuendo **mp** *dim.*

ritard.

intimately con licenza

A tempo *more fully*

glass-es, why then in truth, I pray you find it... I pray you may find_____

p *colla voce (rit.)* **pp** **p**

Più largamente

___ your Foun - tain___ of Youth. I pray you may all_____ find your Foun-tain of

mp **p** > **pp**

Youth.___

pp

8vb

The Gambler's Song
from HELLO OUT THERE

Text adapted from the play by
WILLIAM SAROYAN

Music by
JACK BEESON
(1953)

search - ing the streets for just an - y-bod-y that might be there. You've got to have

some - one___ who's there all the time through win-ter when it

snows, and spring-time when it's pret-ty, and sum-mer-time when it's nice and hot and you can

if you'll come with me____ I won't be wrong_____ an-y more for I'll be

Più allegro ♩ = 104

luck-y. When you've got e-nough mon-ey then you can't be__ wrong an-y more.

You're right____ be-cause the mon-ey says you're right, and I'll have a lot of mon-ey and

you'll be the pret-ti-est girl in all the world._____ And then I'll be proud_ a-round

Fris - co with you on my arm,_ Ka - tey, and all_____ the peo - ple turn - ing

round to look at us!

A Simple Song
from MASS

Text by
STEPHEN SCHWARTZ

Music by
LEONARD BERNSTEIN
(1971)

102

hand,_____ And the sun shall not smite me by day_____ Nor the moon_____ by

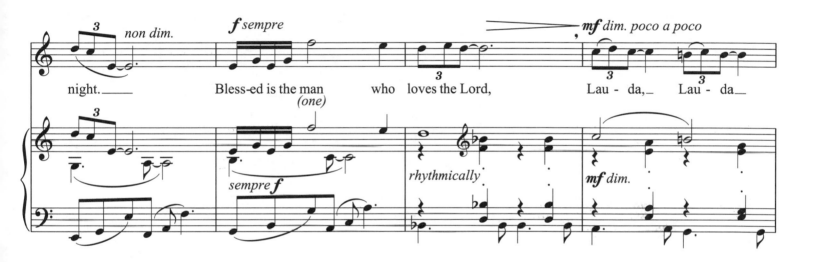

night._____ Bless-ed is the man (one) who loves the Lord, Lau - da,_ Lau - da_

Lau - dē,_ And walks in His ways._____

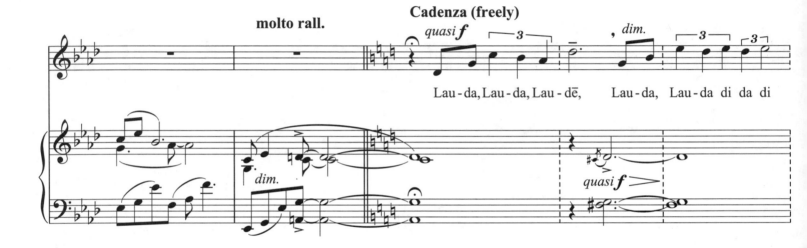

molto rall.

Cadenza (freely)

quasi f   *dim.*

Lau - da, Lau - da, Lau - dē,   Lau - da, Lau - da di da di

dim.

quasi f

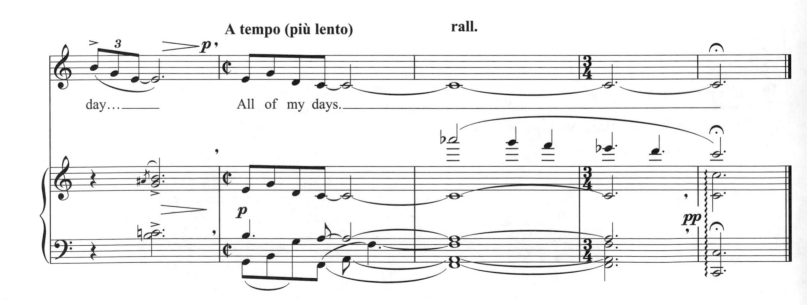

A tempo (più lento)   **rall.**

day...   All of my days.

p

pp

There's a Law (Sam's Aria)

from TROUBLE IN TAHITI
Scene V

Text and Music by
LEONARD BERNSTEIN
(1951)

Allegro non troppo, ma energico ♩. = 88

There are men Who will stud-y the books 'til Judg-ment Day, And ex-am-ine the tech-niques of win-ners ga - lore; There are men Who will prac-tice the rules re - li-gious-ly:___ Ev -'ry day they'll im-prove just a ti - ny bit more: And they'll put all their soul be - hind it; All their e - go, pow-er, drive, and

will and de-sire___ be-hind it, And they'll throw them-selves in:___

But they nev-er will win, they nev-er will win, They nev-er, nev-er, nev-er, nev-er will

win! There's a

law:_____ There's a law a-bout men:_____ There are

men who are flab-by and men who are thin; There are fish who are fat-tish and

fish who are trim in the fin. There are

men Who will sweat out their days in cab-i-nets, And be

pum-meled and bad-gered and beat-en and rolled. There are men Who will

110

112

114

Rucker's Sermon

from COLD SASSY TREE
Act I, Scene 4

Adapted from the novel by
OLIVE ANN BURNS

Text and Music by
CARLISLE FLOYD
(2000)

Allegro moderato ♩ = 96-104

Will, push them chairs t'gether
fer you an' Miss Love since
y'all are th' congregation.

I wanta be sure that folks comin' home
from church know we're havin' church
right here. That'll really set 'em t' talkin'.

Now,

first I want-a talk a-bout re - li-gious zeal. Re - li-gious zeal_____ can be a sick-ness that will

cramp your mind an' shrink yer soul. It's best took in small dos-es or bet-ter still, not at all.

Be-ware of zea-lots 'cause if you

don't see things their way, you're wrong. They don't look kind-ly on those who dif-fer so you

118

wide as th' sky___ that can fill___ with___ joy or with pain,___ so don't mock Me with an emp-ty heart_ 'cause that

says you've_ missed out on life,_____ that you've scorned_ why I put you here.

Meno mosso

When God de-cides my time is up,__ I'll be heart-broke t' turn loose of this world but__ I'll still__ be

grate-ful t' Him that in His wis-dom, His in-fi-nite wis-dom, He put me here.

I've Known I've Loved You

from COLD SASSY TREE
ACT II, Scene 3

Adapted from the novel by
OLIVE ANN BURNS

Text and Music by
CARLISLE FLOYD
(2000)

Lento mosso (♩ = 54)

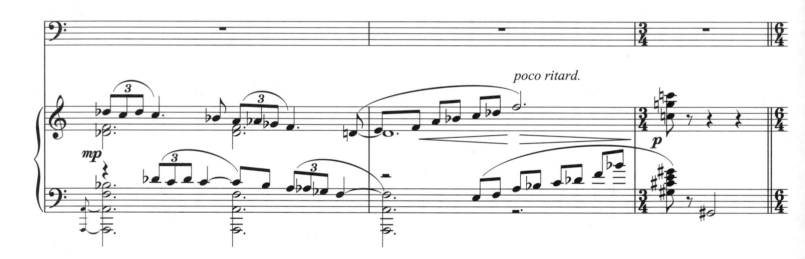

Andante ben misurato (♩ = 74)

I got-ta own up t' some-thin'_ an' it'-ll like-ly drive you off but if I

Poco ritard.

don't there jes' ain't no way I can rest eas-y in my mind.

L'istesso tempo, ma più cantabile

mp

I've known I loved you right__ from th' start, from th' first time I set

p *caloroso*

eyes on you. From that first day you__ come to m' store my

mf

122

A tempo

come here t' live with me. But now they've come back, twice_ as strong. And it

Tempo I

don't do no good t' tell m'-self that I'm too old t' feel sech thangs 'cause m'

heart knows th' truth o' what I feel an' don't hear a word I say. I

love you more than life it-self an' I jes' cain't pre-tend_ no more.

Poco più sostenuto (♩ = 72)

What I want most now, what m' heart is ach-in' for, what I want most in

all th' world, is for you to be a

real wife t' me, t' be a real wife t' me.

I know you cain't nev-er feel th' same, not towards an old man like me.

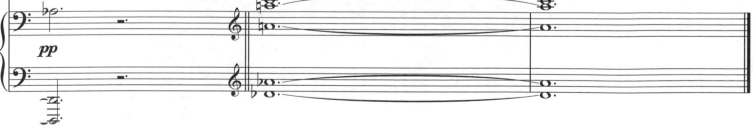

Text adapted from
the novel and play of
JOHN STEINBECK

George's Aria
from OF MICE AND MEN
ACT II

Text and Music by
CARLISLE FLOYD
(1971)

L'istesso tempo più cantabile

Rallentando

Un poco andante e piangendo (♩ = 58)

An un-used ra-zor blade, left be-hind; a worn-out truss and a fad-ed neck-tie; an old har-mon-i-ca and a burnt-out pipe, all that's left to say you've once been a-live.

Risoluto assai (♩ = 69)

No! There's got-ta be more to liv-in' than that! There's just

got-ta be more!_____ I won't set-tle_____ for such a stin-gy life!

I won't set -tle for that! There's just got -ta be some - thin'

more! An' there will be more for

L'istesso tempo, più appassionato

Len-nie an' me!__ There will be more!

Allegro poco maestoso (♩ = 92)

You'll see! I'll nev - er set - tle for this life, we're

not like all____ you lone - some guys.____ We've got our own life, our

own dream.____ We're dif - f'rent: we're not a - lone._____

Sleep, conscience, sleep
from THE PASSION OF JONATHAN WADE
ACT II, Scene 2

Text and Music by
CARLISLE FLOYD
(1962)

Allegro moderato ♩ = 96-104

*(Jonathan seats himself wearily behind his desk.
After a moment he closes his eyes and says very quietly to himself:)*

Adagio mesto (♪ = 96)

poco ritard.

Sleep, con - science, sleep   while

sight - less du - ty o - beys its com - mands.   Sleep, con - science,   slum - ber deep - ly, for   you are the eyes of my

mind and heart and what du - ty must do now you   can - not   see.   Sleep,__ con - science, sleep,   for

du - ty is sight - less, deaf, and mute__ and with - out your eyes it will dumb-ly o - bey.

diminuendo

(He opens his eyes and stands.)

Più mosso (♩. = 48)

Sleep, con - science, I beg you__ to sleep.

mp molto crescendo

Close your fierce, un - blink-ing eyes.__ Don't tor - ment me, leave me__ in peace:

poco f sempre

(He sits once more, closing his eyes,
holding his face in his hands, his voice quiet.)

sleep!_____

Adagio mesto (♪ = 96)

mezzo voce

rallen.

Sleep, con - science, I beg you, sleep.

Close your fierce, pro - test-ing eyes.   Sleep,_____   I beg you to sleep,

stentato

colla voce

(Jonathan suddenly opens his eyes, throws his head back,
and shouts in an agonized voice:)

beg_ you to_ sleep.   Sleep._   Sleep._   SLEEP!_____

Hear Me, Oh Lord
(Blitch's Prayer of Repentance)
from SUSANNAH
ACT II, Scene 4

Text adapted from the play by
WILLIAM SAROYAN

Text and Music by
CARLISLE FLOYD
(1954)

sun comes. Re-turn, O Lord, and hark-en to my plea fer fer-give-ness. Re-

ceive my con-fes-sion, O Lord, an' hear the words o' my re-pent-ance. It's a

hor-ri-ble thing I have done. Fer-give the weak-ness o' my flesh, O Lord, an' con-

demn me not to the e-ter-nal fire fer my sin a-gainst Thee an' the wom-an. She was un-

136

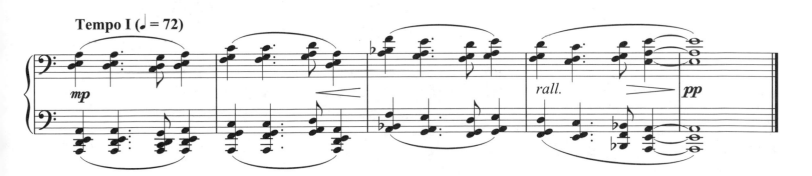

Single bed blanket
(Once upon a time)

from WILLIE STARK
Act I, Scene 2

Text and Music by
CARLISLE FLOYD
(1980)

cov - er the case. Now, the law's like a sin - gle bed blan - ket_____ an'

some poor soul's__ al - ways left out in the cold.__ Now, if

you're the one that's cov-ered by that sin - gle bed blan - ket and are all toast - y warm, on that

cold win - ter night,__ you're not gon - na like all the com - plain - in' you hear from

a tempo

law's like a sin-gle bed blan-ket,_____ an' there's nev-er e-nough to

allarg.   **a tempo**

cov-er the case, but we got-ta keep stretch-in' that blan-ket, Judge,_ to

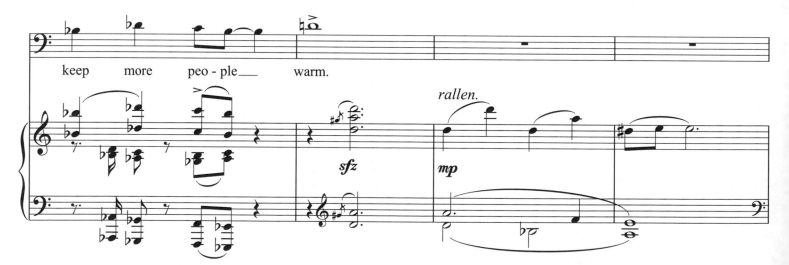

keep more peo-ple__ warm.

rallen.

sfz   *mp*

Più sostenuto ($\text{♩} = 46$)

mp very seriously

ritard.   **a tempo**

Yeah, Judge, I stretch the law. I pull on it hard 'cause I know what it's like to be cold.

p

colla voce   *sfz*

We all come out of the earth

from WILLIE STARK
Act I, Scene 3

Music and Text by
CARLISLE FLOYD
(1980)

Poco più mosso
(♩ = 84)

earth like the oak tree,___ or like the grass. But the

grass and oak tree nev-er___ move;___ they stay all their lives in just one place. But

poco a poco più mosso

man is born to wan-der a-broad, to see new plac-es, new parts of the

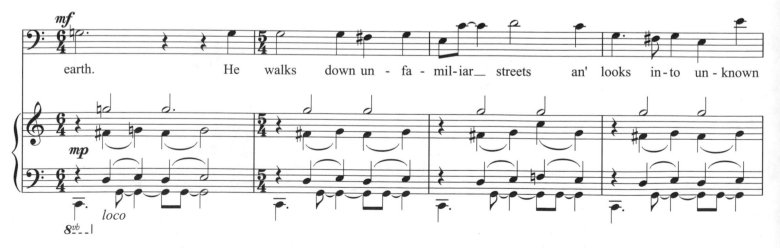

earth. He walks down un-fa-mil-iar___ streets an' looks in-to un-known

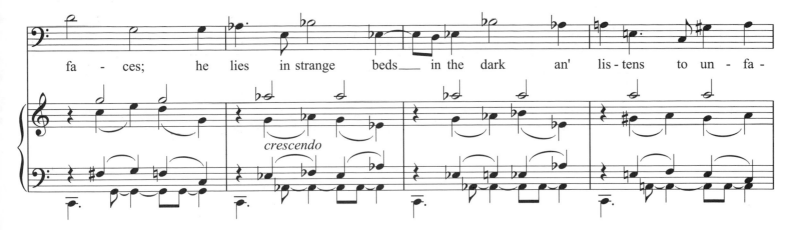

e - ven for - gets who____ he is.____ An' then the hun-ger starts,

a vague an' name - less hun - ger, gnaw-in' at him, gnaw-in' at his heart,

spread-in' through him____ like some ter - ri - ble fe - ver, de - mand - in'____ to be

filled. An' then it comes to him, comes to him that he's

Allegro ma largamente (♩ = 100)

I've got a ram, Goliath
from THE DEVIL AND DANIEL WEBSTER

Text by
STEPHEN VINCENT BENÉT

Music by
DOUGLAS MOORE
(1943)

Poco mosso ♪ = 110

mine._____ I've got a bull, King Ste - phen,__ A bull with a roll - ing eye._____ When he

stamps his foot, the stars come out And the light-en-ing blinks in the sky._____

____ I've got a bull, King Ste - phen,__ With a kick like a can - non ball._____ But he

rit.   a tempo

acts like a suck-ing tur - tle - dove__ When I go in-to his stall._____ I'm not an i - dle

boast-er.___ Let___ this be said of me.___ I was born in old New

Hamp-shire And al-ways fought for the free. They know a-bout Dan - iel

Web - ster Where - ev - er the ea - gle flies,___ And they know he stands for the Un - ion

— And does - n't stand for lies.___ Ask at the work-men's cot-tage,___ Ask at the farm-er's

I cannot still the echo

from THE ROBBERS

Text and Music by
NED ROREM
(1956)

Lento lamentoso (♩ = 63)

I can-not still the ech - o nor

yet shut out the sight.___ I know that I have gone too far, have come too far.___ What

have I done to-night? What am I do-ing here? Is it too late?___

Caught,_____ caught be-tween these two ruth-less fiends and that_

gap - ing_ corpse, it is im - pos - si-ble to leave. The moon_____ like my heart_

_____ has_ ri - sen, and like my heart is sink-ing down__ to - night now.

Caught!_____

When comes the dark - ness of the _ night, and the end _____ of _ strain.

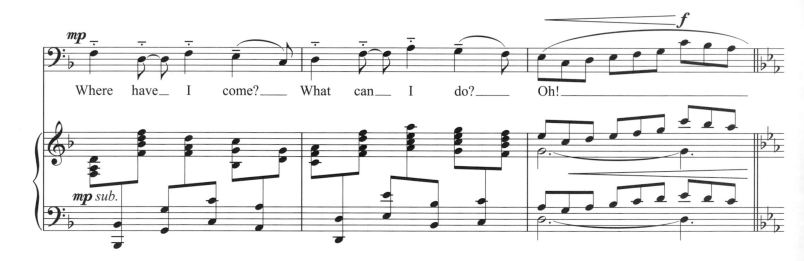

Where have _ I come? _____ What can _ I do? _____ Oh! _____

_____ If I could be as cold as this _ night, as cruel as they are,

I__ would have more gold_____ than__ my share.

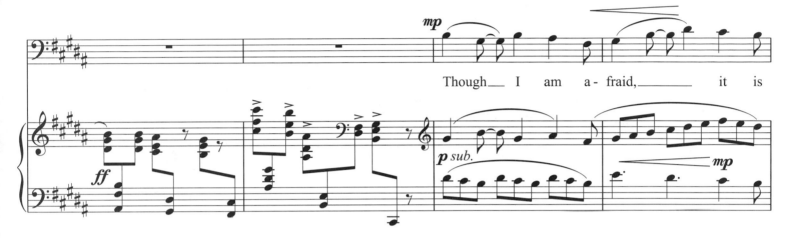

Though__ I am a-fraid,_____ it is

yet no__ ac - ci-dent I let__ my-self__ be__ led._____

What can I do?_____

Where have I come?

half-yelled

Caught!

($\quad$ = 108)

Let my fear lead me now,

and hold my hand, like a hyp-no-tist; it will make me car-ry out my plan.

Nick Shadow's Aria

from THE RAKE'S PROGRESS
Act II, Scene 1

Text by
W.H. AUDEN and
CHESTER KALLMAN

Music by
IGOR STRAVINSKY
(1948-51)

Recitative

(♪ = 120)

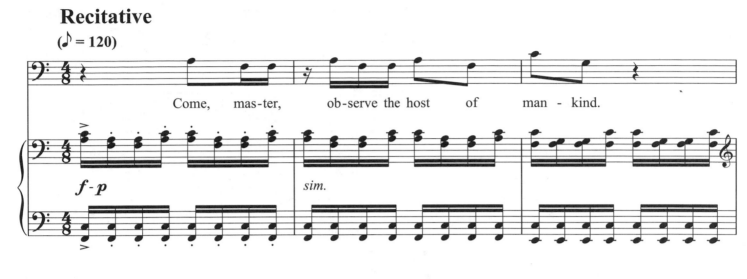

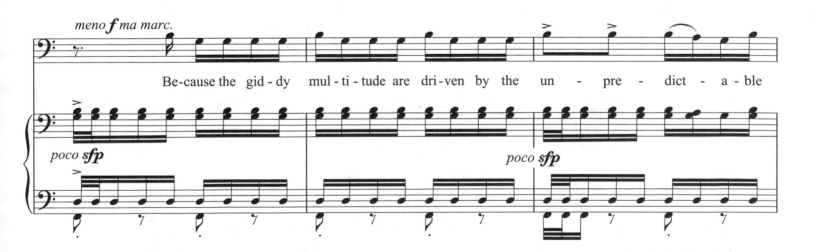

Must of their plea-sures and the so-ber few are

bound by the in-flex-i-ble Ought of their du-ty,

be-tween which slav-er-ies there is no-thing to

choose. Would you be hap-py? Then__ learn to act free-ly. Would you act free-ly?

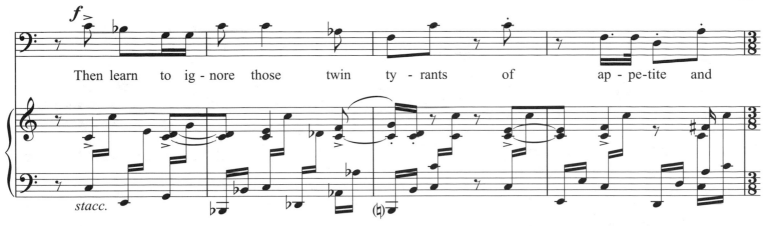

Then learn to ig - nore those twin ty - rants of ap - pe-tite and

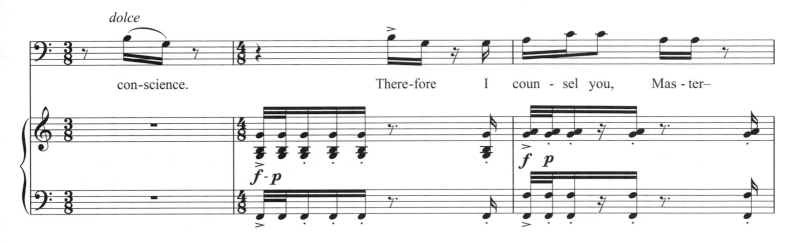

con-science. There-fore I coun - sel you, Mas - ter–

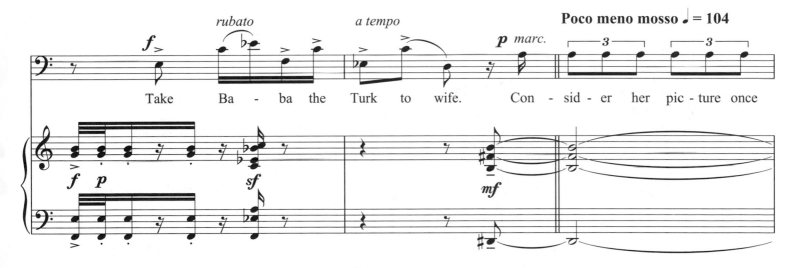

Take Ba - ba the Turk to wife. Con - sid - er her pic - ture once

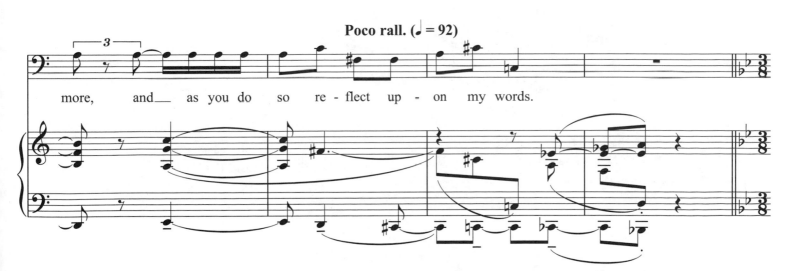

more, and as you do so re - flect up - on my words.

Aria

♪ = 98

In youth the pan-ting slave pur-sues The fair e - va - sive dame;＿ Then, caught in cold-er fet - ters, woos Wealth, Of - fice or a name; Till,

p

stacc.

poco sf

stacc.

old, dis-hon-oured, sick, down-cast____ And fail-ing in his wits,

In Vir-tue's nar-row cell at last The with-ered bonds-man sits.____

That____ man, that man_ a - lone, that

Lyrics:

No eye his fu - ture can fore - tell, No law his past ex -

plain Whom_ nei - ther Pas - sion may com - pel, Nor_

_ Rea - son can re - strain.

Biographies

JOHN ADAMS (b. 1947) is one of America's most admired and frequently performed composers. With his groundbreaking operas *Nixon in China* and *The Death of Klinghoffer*, he brought contemporary history into the opera house for the first time, pioneering an entire genre. *El Niño*, his opera/oratorio on the Nativity, was premiered in Paris in December 2000; like virtually all of his music, it has been recorded on the Nonesuch label, which issued a 10-disc retrospective box set in 1999. Adams's many honors include a Grawemeyer Award for his Violin Concerto (1993) and a Pulitzer Prize in Music for his 2002 score *On the Transmigration of Souls*, commissioned by the New York Philharmonic in commemoration of the first anniversary of the World Trade Center attacks. His opera *Doctor Atomic*, based on the life of J. Robert Oppenheimer and the development of the nuclear bomb, is scheduled to be premiered by San Francisco Opera in September 2005.

DOMINICK ARGENTO (b. 1927) is considered to be America's leading composer of lyric opera. He has written 13 operas which have had major performances in the U.S. as well as Europe. The majority of his music is vocal; all of it—instrumental and vocal—displays a natural dramatic impulse. In a predominantly tonal context, his music freely combines tonality, atonality, and 12-tone writing. Argento studied composition with Nicolas Nabokov and Hugo Weisgall at the Peabody Conservatory, received a Fulbright Fellowship for study with Luigi Dallapiccola and received his PhD from the Eastman School of Music, where he studied with Bernard Rogers. He received two Guggenheim Fellowships (in 1957 and 1964), was awarded the Pulitzer Prize in 1975 for his song cycle *From the Diary of Virginia Woolf*, was a Regents' Professor at University of Minnesota (where he taught for 39 years), and in 2004 won a Grammy for Best Classical Contemporary Composition for his song cycle *Casa Guidi*.

JACK BEESON (b. 1921) studied at the Eastman School of music and with Béla Bartók in New York City. Since 1950 he has composed eight operas in the American vernacular tradition, including *Lizzie Borden*, widely regarded as a classic of the genre. His stage works combine a keen sense of irony with penetrating psychological insight. Beeson's style is wide-ranging, with musical language adapting to realize a distinctive mood, character, or emotion. Vocal music—operas large and small, song cycles, and choral pieces—forms the majority of his output, providing a persuasive outlet for his keen wit and lyrical gifts. Beeson taught at Columbia University for more than three decades.

LEONARD BERNSTEIN (1918–1990) is one of the most widely performed composers of the 20th century. His works successfully bridge the divide between classical and popular idioms; they combine jazz-inspired energy, theatrical panache, and active stylistic eclecticism. His stage works, among them *West Side Story*, *On the Town*, and *Candide*, have become a vital part of the American repertoire. Bernstein's major concert works include three symphonies; *Serenade* for violin, strings, and percussion (1954); *Mass*, commissioned for the opening of the John F. Kennedy Center for Performing Arts in 1971; *Chichester Psalms* for chorus, boy soprano, and orchestra (1974); and *Songfest*, for solo voices and orchestra (1977). He was one of the most admired conductors of the post-war era and played an important role as an educator, including pioneering work on television.

CARLISLE FLOYD (b. 1926) has created a distinctively American idiom for opera, drawing on national folk and religious music traditions. His operas combine penetrating social commentary with acute psychological insight; his sensitive and idiomatic vocal writing has gained the admiration of singers and listeners alike. Floyd writes his own librettos, in which he has treated such themes as the aftermath of the Civil War, the Great Depression, and rural fundamentalism. *Susannah*, his best-known opera, has entered the permanent repertory with countless productions in the U.S. and a growing number in Europe; in recent years, *Of Mice and Men* has achieved great popularity as well. Other significant operas by Floyd include *Willie Stark* (1980), *The Passion of Jonathan Wade* (1962, rev. 1989), and *Cold Sassy Tree* (2000).

DOUGLAS MOORE (1893–1969) earned degrees at Yale University and went on to study composition in Paris with Vincent d'Indy and Nadia Boulanger. His earliest compositions were popular songs, and folk music and rural or pioneer life continued to influence his later works. Moore is best known for his vocal works, particularly the operas *The Devil and Daniel Webster* (1939), *The Ballad of Baby Doe* (1956) and *Giants in the Earth* (1950), for which he won the 1951 Pulitzer Prize. He taught at Barnard College, Columbia University, from 1926 to 1962.

NED ROREM (b. 1923) has been called by *Time* magazine "the world's best composer of art songs"; his evening-length song cycle *Evidence of Things Not Seen* is regarded by many as his magnum opus in the medium. While his vocal writing is justly praised, his output spans nearly every genre: it was an orchestral work, *Air Music*, that earned him the 1976 Pulitzer Prize in Music. His stage works include a full-length opera, *Miss Julie*, plus several chamber operas. Susan Graham and Brian Azawa are among the leading singers who have recorded his music. His recent chamber works have been toured or recorded by the Guarneri String Quartet, the Emerson String Quartet, and the Beaux Arts Trio, among others. He is also a noted author, with 16 books to his credit.

IGOR STRAVINSKY (1882–1971) is widely regarded as the most original and influential composer of the 20th century. He studied with Rimsky-Korsakov in St. Petersburg from 1905–08. His early works were heard by Diaghilev, who commissioned *The Firebird* for Ballets Russes. Further collaborations *Petrushka* and *The Rite of Spring* saw the composer move from nationalism towards vibrant modernism. The wartime period brought a radical, experimental phase; economic conditions prompted smaller-scale theatrical ventures such as *The Soldier's Tale*. *Pulcinella* launched Stravinsky's neo-classical phase which dominated the 1920s–40s. Major works from this period included *Oedipus Rex*, *Symphony of Psalms*, and *The Rake's Progress*. At the outbreak of the Second World War Stravinsky moved to the United States, settling in California. His ballet *Agon* was a watershed for late serial works, including *Requiem Canticles*. Hallmarks of his style in any period include Russian folk inflections, rhythmic energy, and orchestral virtuosity. His ballet scores are among the most significant of the past century.

Conductor **PHILIP BRUNELLE** founded VocalEssence (then known as the Plymouth Music Series) in 1969, leading the organization in its mission to explore the interaction of voices and instruments through innovative programming. His conducting engagements have taken him across the United States, South America, and Europe. He has served on the board of directors of Chorus America and the National Council on the Arts. Currently Brunelle serves on the Board of Regents of St. Olaf College and the Board of Directors of the International Federation for Choral Music. He holds four honorary doctorates as well as honors from the governments of Sweden and Hungary. In 2002 he served as president of the Sixth World Symposium on Choral Music and in 2003 Chorus America honored him with its most prestigious award, the Michael Korn Founder's Award for Development of the Choral Art.

Voice: Baritone/Bass

CD TRACK LISTING

SONJA THOMPSON, PIANO
*PHILIP BRUNELLE, PIANO

CD 1
JOHN ADAMS

1. "Dewain's Song of Liberation and Surprise" from I WAS LOOKING AT THE CEILING AND THEN I SAW THE SKY	4:50
2. "Shake the heavens" from EL NIÑO	2:46
3. "Dawn Air" from EL NIÑO	3:54
4. "News Aria" from NIXON IN CHINA	5:43
5. "Chou En-lai's Epilogue" from NIXON IN CHINA	3:16

DOMINICK ARGENTO

6. "Boor's Aria" from THE BOOR*	2:48
7. "Casanova's Final Air" from CASANOVA'S HOMECOMING*	3:06
8. "Sly's Aria" from CHRISTOPHER SLY*	2:10
9. "Metatron's Sermon" from THE MASQUE OF ANGELS*	6:25
10. "Ralph's Letter-Ballad" from THE SHOEMAKERS' HOLIDAY*	3:52
11. "Simon's Aria" from THE SHOEMAKERS' HOLIDAY*	3:07
12. "The Lecturer" from A WATER BIRD TALK*	2:18

JACK BEESON

13. "Prescription for Living" from DR. HEIDEGGER'S FOUNTAIN OF YOUTH	3:44
14. "The Gambler's Song" from HELLO OUT THERE	3:01

CD 2
LEONARD BERNSTEIN

1. "A Simple Song" from MASS	3:30
2. "There's a law" from TROUBLE IN TAHITI	3:28

CARLISLE FLOYD

3. "Rucker's Sermon" from COLD SASSY TREE	3:47
4. "I've known I've loved you" from COLD SASSY TREE	4:08
5. "George's Aria" from OF MICE AND MEN	3:14
6. "Sleep, conscience, sleep" from THE PASSION OF JONATHAN WADE	4:02
7. "Hear me, O Lord" from SUSANNAH	3:19
8. "Single bed blanket" from WILLIE STARK	2:30
9. "We all come out of the earth" from WILLIE STARK	4:47

DOUGLAS MOORE

10. "I've got a ram, Goliath" from THE DEVIL AND DANIEL WEBSTER	2:39

NED ROREM

11. "I cannot still the echo" from THE ROBBERS	3:17

IGOR STRAVINSKY

12. "Nick Shadow's Aria" from THE RAKE'S PROGRESS	2:58

Recorded at Studio M, Minnesota Public Radio, St. Paul, Minnesota
Tom Mudge, engineer